# My African S

Mike and Clair

To 'old' India hands from an old
Africa hand!

I hope you enjoy these tales of
my misspent youth.

With kindest regards

Tony Goddard.

2nd October 2010.

# My African Stories

*by*

A J Goddard

The Memoir Club

First published in 2005 by
The Memoir Club
Stanhope Old Hall
Stanhope
Weardale
County Durham

British Library Cataloguing in
Publication Data.
A catalogue record for this book
is available from the
British Library

ISBN: 1 84104 121 1

Typeset by TW Typesetting, Plymouth, Devon
Printed and bound by Antony Rowe Ltd, Eastbourne

*For my son Glyn and the other members
of the tribe of Goddard*

# Contents

# List of Illustrations

# Preface

'Did I ever tell you how I did a star turn as a dancer at the Grand Independence Ball when I was a Resident Magistrate in the South Western Province of what used to be Northern Rhodesia?' I asked rhetorically.

My wife, Gill, the other end of the table stirred uneasily.

'Not another of your African stories.'

'The District Commissioner (a splendid fellow from Stoke on Trent) and I were invited to attend the Ball which was organised by our African clerks and we were the only Europeans there,' I continued remorselessly. 'I was invited to choose a record to dance to and asked for the Beatles. What I didn't know was that I was, as a result, the only one allowed to dance. I accordingly found myself, and the African damsel whom I persuaded to join me, the only couple on the floor doing the Twist. All was going well, and we were cheered to the echo, until I discovered that my trousers had split in a distinctly awkward place and I had to leave the floor, metaphorically speaking, with my tail between my legs.'

My audience, well wined-and-dined dinner guests, were kind enough to applaud my tale and my wife, relieved by the applause and having heard the story only three or four times before, was moved to suggest that 'You really should write your stories down sometime' leaving unspoken the implied condition 'and thereafter refrain from ever telling them again.'

I ignored her suggestion, as any experienced husband usually ignores his wife's suggestions, which require effort on his part. My determination not to do so was reinforced by the fact that I had not kept a diary during my time in the Colonial Service (and despite my father's advice that if I kept a diary it would one day keep me) so that I only had my memory to rely on.

And then my first wife, Ursula, looked out the old photographs that we had taken during our three years in an outstation in Northern Rhodesia (now Zambia) and I thought I jolly well would set down all of my African stories . . . and here they are.

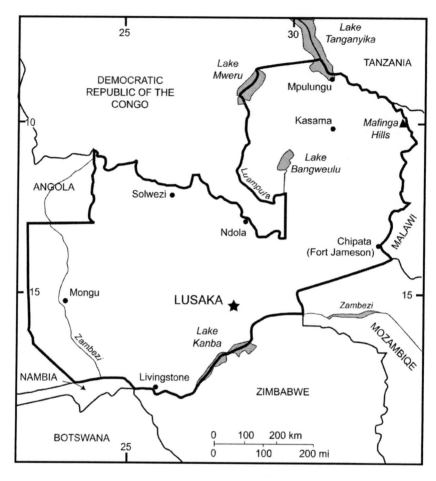

*Northern Rhodesia (Zambia) and its neighbours*

# Acknowledgements

To Ursula for her part in these adventures; to my good friend Kendal McDonald without whose help and encouragement this book would not have seen the light of day; and of course to my wife Gill for her patience and for having to listen to my African stories.

# CHAPTER 1

# Schooldays

M Y FATHER RETURNED from the war with a 'Mentioned in Dispatches' for his part in organising the Yalta Conference, and with no mind to return to the now socialist Bristol City council where, before the war, he had been employed as a lawyer in the town clerk's department (although he remained a proud pupil barrister and a member of Grays's Inn until his death). Instead he took a teacher training course and was recruited into the Education Department of the Government of Northern Rhodesia. Northern Rhodesia (now the Republic of Zambia) was at the time a British Colony and administered as such by the Colonial Office in London which recruited and dispatched young men to run the country in the name of the Crown (at that time George VI) who was represented in Northern Rhodesia by a Governor who on high days and holidays wore a splendid hat with an ostrich feather in it.

Northern Rhodesia, like its smaller but noisier neighbour Southern Rhodesia (now Zimbabwe) had, as its name implies, been incorporated by Cecil Rhodes, as part of his empire-building frenzy, into his British South Africa Company. Subsequently in 1924, and again following the example of its southern neighbour, it was taken over and administered by the Colonial Office. This process of colonisation was considerably encouraged by the arrival in the country during this period of European Missionaries of various denominations of which David Livingstone was the first.

Geographically Northern Rhodesia was situated on a plateau between three thousand and four thousand feet above sea level in virtually the middle of Africa. Starting in the north with what was then the Belgian Congo and is now the Democratic Republic of the Congo and moving clockwise its neighbours were, in the east, Tanganyika (now Tanzania), Nyasaland (now Malawi) and, for a short distance in the south-east, Mozambique. In the south, as one might expect, there was Southern Rhodesia. Moving up the other side of the clock face was Botswana and then Namibia's narrow Caprivi Strip between Botswana in the west and Angola in the north-west. After that one was back to the Congo. The country was occupied by Bantu people, who moved down from the north during the Iron Age, pushing out the original smaller Bushmen-type people. There were various tribes, approximately, but not exactly, coinciding with the seven provinces into which the country was divided for administrative purposes.

The climate of Northern Rhodesia was on the whole very good as a result of being so high, with the exception of the river valleys such as the Luangwa and Zambezi. The 'rainy' season, as it was always called, started in December and continued until April after which it became dry and pleasant. Starting in August it became increasingly and unpleasantly hot so that the rains in December were a relief, bringing the hot weather to an end. The combination of heat and damp made for humidity and an immediate bursting into life of both plants and animals. The rains also made the roads, which were predominantly simply graded and compacted earth, virtually impassable.

The country is large, about the size of the United Kingdom and France combined (according to the guide-book). It is for the most part a kind of savannah, that is, grassland dotted to a varying degree with trees and bushes and usually referred to as 'the Bush' or more graphically, to describe the vast area of undistinguished grassland across which we crawled on the diabolical roads, 'miles and miles of bloody Africa.' The majority of the population, certainly in my father's time, lived in villages out in the Bush, practising a simple form of subsistence agriculture. The main sources of the country's wealth were the copper and other mines in the centre of the country, known as the 'Copper Belt' in which the managerial class was predominantly recruited from Southern Rhodesia or South Africa.

How or why my father joined the Colonial Service and elected for Northern Rhodesia I do not know, but in any event 1946 found my mother, with my brother and me, travelling, in troop ship conditions, on one of the Union Castle boats, with all of the household goods in the hold, on her way to join my father who had flown on ahead. I have very little recollection of the journey save of the Custom sheds at Cape Town where the passengers, mainly women and most with children, exhausted from wartime Britain, and an unpleasant two-week journey, were kept through a whole day from the early morning until the train up-country left in the evening in the heat, while relays of Afrikaans Customs and Immigration officers did their unpleasant best to humiliate and delay them. I have a clear recollection of arriving in the dark in Lusaka, the capital of Northern Rhodesia, to be met by my father in a second-hand American car. (American cars were thought to stand up better to the earth roads than the smaller English cars of the period.)

There was a strong whiff of the 'wild west' about Lusaka in those days. We dismounted from the train, which had the same veranda at each end of the carriage as did the trains of the wild west, not onto a raised platform but onto raw sand – a long climb down for those with short legs or hampered with luggage and tired from the five-day train journey. The town, as we discovered in daylight, had as its commercial centre a single line of shops running parallel to and separated from the railway line by a hundred yards of rough bush intersected by the tracks made by the feet of the local Africans. The shops were similar to those familiar with cowboy films, mainly single-storied with a wide roof projecting out over a raised pavement to give shade to the shop and the customers passing by and to an apparently large proportion of the local African male population who had nothing better to do than to loll in the shade of the sidewalk.

The road, which was heavily cambered, was metalled in its very centre but the steep slopes either side, where there was room to park at an angle to the pavement, were not. There were deep ditches both sides of the road to dispose of storm water and those ditches, taken with the steep camber of the road, made parking a distinct hazard for the unwary, such as my mother who set about learning to drive. The shops or stores, as they were more properly called, were mainly, but not entirely, Indian-owned. There was also a substantial Indian township and shopping centre set at right angles to the main street and just off the embryo avenue which ran uphill from one end of the main street to the Law Courts and Government offices. From there the road ran along a handsome, established avenue through some pleasant woodland and the European residential areas, to a most handsome brick-built Government House on the very edge of the township but conveniently close to the Lines of the Northern Rhodesia Regiment.

Our destination was Munali, a large secondary school which lay down a side turning, off the avenue, just before it reached Government House and down past the boundary of the Northern Rhodesia Regiment barracks and training area. My father's first posting was as a teacher to what was at the time the only secondary school in the territory. In those days it took the boys (I cannot recollect any girls) years to grind their way through the primary school system and qualify for a place at secondary school. They had then to beg or borrow the money to support themselves through their senior schooling. Bearing in mind that the young hopefuls came from all over the country and were, in most cases, many days travelling away from home and the support of their families, it must have been only the most determined who completed the course. By the time they had done so they were young adults in their early twenties.

My father appeared to love the work. His enthusiasm was obviously appreciated as, in later years, when I followed his example and joined the Colonial Service in Northern Rhodesia, I found that my surname carried considerable prestige with many of the senior civil servants and ministers in the new independent regime that was taking over and who had been students of my father's at Munali. We were given a marvellous two-storey house at the edge of the school campus, a corner house overlooking the Regiment's assault course and parade-ground.

My father had been told that the schooling in Northern Rhodesia was of a European standard and adequate to allow my brother and me to go on, in due course, to an English Public School, without the need to go first to a preparatory school. My parents had in mind Clifton College in Bristol where my mother's family would be available to look after us during the holidays. The local schools were in the event less than adequate and accordingly, at the age of nine, I was packed off to Kingswood School in Grahamstown in South Africa for the last year of my father's first three-year tour. I remember little of the year save that I found that closer acquaintance with South Africans did little to change the opinion I had formed of them in the Customs sheds in Capetown. I seem to have spent a large part of my time at school in South Africa fighting them, earning my housemaster's nickname 'my little Admiral', reflecting the fact that, in addition to being unusually belligerent, I was also the smallest boy in the school. Looking back I have to confess to having no good memories of my time there but only some little satisfaction at having survived a testing experience.

Alas for my parents' hopes! When at the end of their first tour they returned to England and touted my brother and me around the Public Schools, with a view to my starting when they returned at the end of their second tour (when I would have been thirteen), they were told in no uncertain terms that a sketchy knowledge of Afrikaans was not going to assist me with the Common Entrance Exam which required, in those days, at least a rudimentary knowledge of Latin and a European language, neither of which figured in the South African school syllabus until a much later stage, if at all.

Although they were booked to return to Northern Rhodesia taking my brother and me with them (in addition to my sister Mary who had by then joined the family) they decided, only a week or so before the date of their return, that there was no alternative, if my brother and I were to qualify for an English Public School, but for us to be sent to an English preparatory school, with immediate effect, to prepare us for the Common Entrance Exam which was the hurdle over which all those boys who willingly or unwillingly wanted to go to a Public school had to jump.

The preparatory school chosen for us was owned and run by a splendid old gentleman. A distinguished Classics scholar with a well-known Latin Primer and the editorship of some of *Caesar's Commentaries* to his credit, he was a keen cricketer and rugby player and had had an adventurous time in the First World War with the Rifle Brigade 'in which I had the honour to serve', as he invariably added. He had been shot through the throat in the first battle of the Somme, fortunately, as he would comment, or he would otherwise have undoubtedly been killed in the second, in which his unit took very heavy casualties.

Although undoubtedly a kind-hearted man, his teaching methods would horrify a modern teacher. He operated on the premise that all boys, until at least the age of thirteen, had the characteristics of puppy dogs and were to be treated as such. He also believed that we worked better under pressure so that his Latin classes were as much a battle of wits as a process of imbibing knowledge, with a clout on the side of the head or a few strokes of the cane as the penalty for failure. Boys, like puppy dogs, have their wiles and our copies of the *Commentaries* were often handed down from one generation of boys to the next, accumulating in the process all kinds of valuable graffiti – not only the translation of the more obscure words but key words which would prompt a question and hopefully cause a delay which would avoid the need to do any more translation. I remember for instance that the question 'Please Sir, what does *levis* mean?' was good for twenty minutes on the difference between the heavily-armed Roman legionnaire and the lightly-armed scouts (*levis*), complete with an enumeration of the kit of the respective troops and a comparison with the marching order and scouting order of a private in the Rifle Brigade during the Great War. I am not sure it was the best way of inculcating a love of the classics in us but it undoubtedly taught us to keep our heads under pressure. To the Major's surprise and, I suspect, regret, I completed my time at his school without ever feeling the oft-threatened cane, although it came perilously close on occasions. This, however, was as nothing to his surprise, or for that matter mine, that I succeeded in passing my Common Entrance with one point to spare to qualify for Radley, the Public School of my parents' choice.

We did not see my parents at all during the two and a half years of their second tour, spending our holidays with grandparents, but soon after the start of their second tour my mother insisted that my brother and I (my sister was of course too young to send away to school) should fly out for our long summer holiday. The journey out to Africa in those days was still something of an adventure. We travelled by flying boat from Southampton water to Lake Victoria, I think it must have been, and thence by Land-Rover to Nairobi where we were to transfer to an ordinary plane to fly down Africa to meet our parents in Lusaka. We flew BOAC, whose boast it was that 'We look after you'. At Victoria Bus Station in London, where we checked in, we were placed by an aunt into the custody of one of the air-hostesses, nice sensible middle-class girls with good accents, who whisked us onto the luxury coach for the journey to Southampton where we were to join the flying boat for an *overnight* (this in reverent tones) flight as far as Rome. We arrived at Southampton in the early evening where we had a large meal, complete with silver service, in a most superior hotel overlooking Southampton water where the flying boat, looking like a silver duck, was made ready to receive us. The air-hostess appointed to supervise our doings helped us through dinner, ordering for us and assisting our choice from the impressive array of cutlery before us. Later she remained in close attendance as we boarded the motorboat, which took us out to the flying boat, and subsequently during the exhilarating departure in a veil of white water and then the stately flight in the dark across the channel and the continent to Rome.

Beyond Rome it was impossible to travel at night and so, after refuelling there the next morning, we continued our stately progress across the Mediterranean to Cairo where we must have spent a second night because I remember us taking our seats in the early dawn for the long flight up the Nile to Khartoum. The Captain, resplendent in a white uniform and with a large RAF moustache, making his way up the cabin, having been supervising the loading through the door at the rear, I presume, noticed my brother and me (the only children on the flight) and asked if we had ever seen the Pyramids before. I admitted that we had not. 'All right,' he said, 'after we take off, I'll do a couple of turns around the Pyramids so that you can see them. Keep a good look out of your window.' Breathlessly we promised we would do so and, sure enough, soon after we had taken off, the flying boat made a couple of circuits so that we could see the Pyramids and the Sphinx in all their glory, with the sun coming up over the horizon, just beginning to bathe them in light. A minute later the Captain returned to check that we had indeed seen the sight before straightening up and heading on up the Nile.

We spent a third night at Khartoum of which I remember little except coming ashore in a motor boat in the dusk and seeing the palm trees standing out on the bank clear against the darkening sky and the hot steamy and very 'foreign' kind of heat and smell that made me rather homesick. We landed on a lake near Nairobi the next day where we left the flying boat and were taken by Land-Rover to the Norfolk Hotel where it was discovered that there was some problem with our onward connection. There was a suggestion that the air-hostess would devote the next day to looking after us but, young as we were, it was so patently obvious that she had other plans of her own that we assured her that we would be perfectly happy on our own. And so, having been installed in our room, we duly repaired to the dining room where we took dinner on our own amongst all the adults and thereafter returned to our room where we read our books, with which, as always, we were well supplied, and then went to bed. We took breakfast the next day and asked at Reception if they had any news of our further travel arrangements. No one seemed to know anything about us and so we set off to explore the town.

We eventually found our way to the market where we spent some time haggling for and buying the particularly good wooden animals that the local Africans carved, which presupposes that we must have changed some money at Reception. We returned to the hotel for lunch, half expecting that some one would ask how long we expected to be eating there without payment, and afterwards returned to our room to read again. At suppertime we presented ourselves at the dining room and again no questions were asked. Next morning we asked again at Reception about our onward travel arrangements with no result and so once again we went out to explore the town. When we returned at lunch-time, however, it was to find that there was something of a panic about us. Authority had eventually been goaded into activity, by a stream of anguished telegrams from my parents enquiring what BOAC had done with their sons aged thirteen and ten who had failed to arrive on the flight they had been booked on and had been missing somewhere in Central Africa for nearly two days. Authority had to admit that they had taken custody of us at Victoria Coach station and had carried us as far as Nairobi but had no record of what had happened to us after that. They were accordingly extremely relieved when we reported to Reception who put two and two together and made haste to get us on the first available flight to Northern Rhodesia. There our distraught mother, in an effort to calm her worries about her missing sons, had passed the hours making Christmas puddings and ignoring the fact that it was in the middle of the hot season.

In any event we had a splendid holiday with my parents in Fort Jameson, the capital of the Eastern Province where my father was the Provincial Education Officer. In the expectation of our arrival, he had saved up his touring in the backwoods to visit some of his more distant schools so that we could join him. Thus it was that little primary schools out in the wilds of the Luangwa valley, who could safely have expected to remain in decent obscurity, would suddenly find themselves the sometimes reluctant recipients of a formal but entirely unexpected visit from the Provincial head of their department. One of the problems with the schools was not enforcing attendance (on the contrary the schools were oversubscribed) but preventing parents enrolling children before the age at which they could properly attend school. It must have been difficult for the teacher, in the absence of birth certificates and in a village which was not his own, to know which, in an eager line of children, was or was not over the magic age of five. It was hardly surprising that under pressure of parents, anxious that their child should make an early start on the all–important educational ladder, the headmaster should give the young applicants the benefit of the doubt. It was my father's unenviable task to audit the master's decisions and exclude such of the children as were more obviously under age. His test, heaven alone knows where he acquired it, was to ask any child of whom he had suspicions, to touch his or her left ear with the fingers of the right hand. Conveniently it appeared that only a child over the age of five is able to do this. How long the children remained excluded after our departure was another matter.

On these trips we travelled in a baby lorry known as a Vanette and were escorted by my father's Government driver and the new cook, Joey. Joey had been recruited in Fort Jameson, he being of the Ngoni tribe who were said to be an offshoot of the Zulus who had trekked north to get out of the bloodshed in South Africa brought about by Chaka, the Zulu Emperor. Normally we stayed overnight in the little rural rest houses that the Government maintained for their officers on tour. In District Headquarters these would be quite civilised, with a permanent staff to do the cooking and with stores of tins and basic foodstuffs available for sale. Out in the bush, however, the rest houses provided little more than a roof and some very rudimentary furniture for the traveller. We children loved it all and particularly the fact that we had, perforce, to sit in the back of the Vanette with Joey in nests amongst the luggage. In those days the areas that we toured were, on occasions, so remote that many of the local people, although they had seen adult Europeans before in the person of the various Government officers who toured from time to time around the villages, had never seen European children. My five-year-old sister particularly was the centre of much interest and comment.

It was on the way by air from Fort Jameson to Lusaka on the first leg of our journey back to school that I recall an incident that was pretty typical of the internal flights in that era. My brother and I were flying in one of the many versions of the Dakota, that seemed to dominate the internal routes, when the door at the rear, a couple of rows behind where we were sitting, flew open. The aircraft was not, of course, pressurised and so no great harm was done, although the noise was quite impressive and a fair amount of alarm and despondency was caused to the passengers. The single-handed air-hostess flew up the aisle to the cockpit where we heard her shout above the noise of the wind to the Captain that the door had flown open and what was she to do about it. The aircraft was at the time experiencing a fair amount of turbulence and the Captain obviously reckoned that he had enough on his plate without having to deal with closing doors and panicky air-hostesses and we heard him shout in reply, 'Then shut the bloody thing, you stupid woman.' The poor woman straightened up and turned back into the passenger compartment. Putting on an ingratiating smile, she walked down the aircraft looking for assistance and wisely picked on two large young men in the seats immediately in front of us. She stopped by them. 'Would you please be so kind as to close the door for me?' we heard her ask brightly, as if this was a perfectly usual request. The young men seemed to regard the request in the same light and rose at once to do her bidding. 'I'll hold your belt,' one said to the other and craning our necks we could see one young man hold on to the back of a seat with one arm while he held his companion's thick leather belt with the hand of the other. Thus secured, the other young man leaned out and eventually succeeded in grappling the errant door and pulling it shut.

Back at home I returned to Radley College just outside Abingdon in Berkshire (but only five miles or so from Oxford) where two years later I was joined by my far more intelligent and hard-working brother with a scholarship under his belt. I thoroughly enjoyed my time at Radley, which was, I consider, a very good school. From what I have seen and heard of it, it is probably an even better school now than it was in my time. It is best known, I guess, as a rowing school with the benefit of having easy access to a long stretch of the River Thames, and its crews compete regularly at Henley and other national regattas.

Although I had achieved the standard at Common Entrance sufficient to satisfy Radley's admittedly exacting requirements and although I had sailed into the A stream in rugby football and rowing, my academic prowess entitled me to a seat definitely 'below the salt'. As I had never had any pretensions to scholarship, my place in the academic B stream suited me very well, as I found I could comfortably maintain my position in the middle of the lower classes with the minimum of effort. Thus it was that I acquired a bare minimum of O levels (excluding elementary mathematics) and, with my reputation for stupidity well documented, I settled down to enjoy rugby and rowing for the remainder of my school career. Fortunately, or unfortunately as I considered at the time, I fell into the hands of an inspirational young master. In his recent past a distinguished scrum half, he was the master in charge of rugby and, with an eccentric style all of his own, taught arts subjects in the middle reaches of the school.

As a matter of policy I always sat at the front, directly under the master's eye. I had found that in that position I escaped his gaze and questions, which tended to be directed to those classmates who preferred to skulk in the back row. Thus it was that for the best part of a term I continued to float serenely in the bosom of the academic 'also rans' until one cataclysmic hot afternoon, as I drowsed in one of the lessons, the master rapped out a question to the class. Half asleep, I instinctively rapped out the correct reply. There was a pregnant pause while he studied me and I tried to resume my usual expression of industrious imbecility. Eventually he said 'Gaddud.' It was one of his idiosyncrasies that he always referred to God as Gad. 'I have a feeling that you have been fooling me and that you are more intelligent than you let on.' And then those ominous words 'and from now on I will be keeping a close eye on you' and he did. As luck would have it he not only remained one of my masters for the remainder of the term but became my form master for the whole of the next year. I cannot pretend that I ever became an academic heavyweight but under his combined goading and encouragement I passed into the A level class where I succeeded in getting A levels of a sufficient standard, in arts subjects at least, to contemplate applying for a university place.

The same could not be said of elementary mathematics. In those days I believe one could take O levels twice a year. On every occasion that I could I presented myself to the examiners in elementary mathematics and every time they rejected me. Thus it was that as an eighteen-year-old and Head of House (or Social as Radley called their houses) and a senior member of the First Rugby Fifteen I sat two or three times a week among the less mathematically gifted of the fourteen- and fifteen-year-olds to try, unsuccessfully, to absorb enough knowledge of elementary mathematics to satisfy the examiners. In mitigation I should add that for a large part of the time the teaching was, shall we say, less than inspired. Indeed the main claim to fame of the master involved seemed to me to be that he had been the headmaster of a school in Ceylon. As one of his colleagues unkindly remarked, however, 'I imagine anyone can be a headmaster in Ceylon if one can be bothered to go all the way out there.'

I had decided to be a lawyer when I was fourteen years old. Whether this was because it was my father's ambition one day to qualify as a barrister or whether I was impressed by our solicitor guardian or just felt it was the right profession for me, I cannot now remember. In any event it had the advantage that it saved me having to give any thought to what I should do once my education was completed. From that decision it also followed that I needed to go to university. As Radley was so close to Oxford and as my father had been offered a scholarship to Balliol College to read History (which family circumstances prevented his taking up), there was never any question where I should go to complete my education. I accordingly presented myself for extra coaching with a view to sitting some scholarship-level papers and College Entrance Exams.

I confess, however, that the study did not come easily and I found it all too easy to be diverted to attending to the duties which my promotion to Head of House and Second Head of School brought with it. Happily, however, St Edmund Hall (always known as Teddy Hall), the Oxford College of my choice, at that time operated a somewhat eccentric but very effective entrance policy. Instead of recruiting solely on the basis of examination results, they had the enlightened idea of taking only one third of the intake of undergraduates as a result of their exam results. One third they unashamedly recruited as sportsmen. For the remaining third they recruited young men (there were of course no women in college in those days) who were in the opinion of the selection committee 'good chaps' and likely to add something to the life of the college. Happily my housemaster was grateful to me for what he considered I had done to improve the standing of the House and, as an alumnus of the college, persuaded his old chum the admissions tutor to give me a place. I had hoped that this success was due to my prowess on the rugby field but in reality I believe it had more to do with the need of the boat club for an additional oarsman and my housemaster's connections. My place was, however, dependent on my passing elementary mathematics at Responsions. Responsions were a special type of examination operated in those days by Oxford for the assistance of those, mainly sportsmen, to whom the colleges wanted to offer places, but who had difficulty in acquiring the necessary minimum of O levels. To them, as to me, the colleges offered Responsions in the same basic subjects as the usual O levels but reputed to be at a slightly lower standard. It suffices to say that I spent the summer after leaving school attending classes in mathematics with a formidable old lady in North Oxford. It worked, however, and my pass in the subject was posted the day before I had to present myself to take up my place at Oxford to read for a degree in Law of the Honours School of Jurisprudence.

I enjoyed Oxford particularly after being recruited into the boat club my second term. Rowing thereafter dominated my life at Oxford and it was particularly helpful during the Vacations. With my parents abroad I had no base to which to take myself and my dirty washing at the end of term and no one to sponge off for a few weeks to allow the bank balance to recover. It was therefore very helpful that the boat club often 'came up' (returned to college), usually on preferential terms, a week or so early or 'went down' (left college) a week or so after the formal end of term.

There was also the bonus, certainly one year and it may have been two, that the well-known riverside hotel, the Swan at Streatley, put the first crew up for ten days before the start of the summer term so that we could train in seclusion and comfort before the term began. Looking back on it I suppose that as we were at the time the Head of the River crew at Oxford they may have derived some prestige from having our boat on trestles on their lawn. I only recall with gratitude that they provided us with a comfortable bed and three meals a day at a cost of exactly one pound per man per day.

I was fortunate to have joined the boat club at the same time as the college had recruited the major part of the school crew that had just won the Princess Elizabeth cup at Henley Regatta. The core membership of the club was very small but we rowed together for the next three years and dominated Oxford rowing during that period. In fact no crew in which I rowed during the whole of my time at Oxford was ever beaten by any other Oxford College crew. None of us was well off and we were reduced to contributing to buy an extremely dilapidated builder's van to transport us to Wolvercote where we kept our boat and did our training.

This took us through North Oxford, inhabited, at least by repute, by Oxford University dons and their wives and widows. Our dilapidated van caused some obviously amused looks from other road users until we took to putting a notice in the back window, with type just large enough to be read by a vehicle close behind, bearing the legend 'DON'T LAUGH MADAM YOUR DAUGHTER MAY BE IN HERE.'

It was during the summer vacation at the end of my second year at Oxford that my parents scrimped and saved to fly the three of us out to Kasama in the Northern Province, where my father was the Provincial Education Officer. By this time my brother had joined me at Teddy Hall, where in due course his degree proved that, in contrast to me, he fitted his rowing around his work rather than his work around his rowing. My sister had also been sent to school in England and was at Wycombe Abbey where she later became deputy head girl.

It was a splendid holiday. My father, as one of the senior officers on the station, had a lovely old-style bungalow right on the golf course (all provincial headquarters and most district headquarters boasted a golf course, usually with nine holes and with sand greens). There was an active amateur dramatic society which put on *The Ghost Train* in which I was bullied into taking part. Above all there was the Provincial Commissioner's swimming pool. Sometime in the not too distant but more understanding past, a former Provincial Commissioner must have been a keen gardener. The result was a wonderful garden extending, I guess, over several acres around the official residence. The crowning glory of the garden was a large swimming pool, artistically set into the valley which ran down through the garden, and surrounded by flowers and shrubs. I have no doubt that it had originally appeared in the accounts as a reservoir but certainly by our time it had long since ceased to be used for that purpose and was used solely for the most welcome refreshment of the Provincial Commissioner, his family and friends. We were very fortunate that the incumbent at the time of our visit was Len Bean and he and his wife Nancy, being warm-hearted New Zealanders, were apparently happy to allow the children of the expatriate officers on the station to make free with the pool. I suppose it also provided company for their daughter Jenny, who was just about the same age as my sister. And so it was that the pool became the social centre for a host of young people for most of the day, most days during the long summer holiday. And very much we enjoyed it.

The Bean family had been close friends of my parents for most of my parents' time in Africa and against that background it was suggested that

I should coach Jenny in elementary mathematics, a competence which she required to enable her to follow her mother's example and become a nurse. The irony of my teaching anyone mathematics was so exquisite that I feel sure the idea must have come from my father. In any event for an hour or so three or four times a week I would lead the occasionally rebellious Miss Bean into the house and attempt to instil such rudiments of very elementary mathematics as I could remember. Whether or not my coaching had anything to do with it, the fact is that Jenny did, in due course, pass whatever examination she needed and the Beans were duly grateful.

Another pleasant interlude was touring with Derek Goodfellow of whom I later saw a great deal. Northern Rhodesia had recently (in 1953) been joined with Southern Rhodesia and Nyasaland into the Central African Federation of which Roy Walensky was the forceful prime minister. The theory behind the project was that it would provide a format for local multiracial self-rule. It was popular with the European settlers, of which there were many more in Southern than Northern Rhodesia, who saw it as a step on the way to taking over Government from Whitehall. The African population in Northern Rhodesia saw it (no doubt correctly) as an impediment to universal suffrage and African rule. The expatriate civil servants were deeply suspicious of it on the basis that it would bleed the copper wealth of the North for the benefit of the European-dominated South. Against that political background the Federation decided to make a substantial investment in the development of the underdeveloped parts of Northern Rhodesia. As the largest, poorest and certainly the most vocal of the Provinces, the Northern Province, the home of Kenneth Kaunda (the leader of the most militant of the Nationalist parties) was chosen as the recipient of this welcome largesse. Anxious to ensure that it received its fair share of the fund, every Government Department sent its most persuasive officers post-haste to the North, where the allocation of the fund was in the hands of a distinguished civil servant. As this gentleman possessed a mane of white hair he was immediately nicknamed Father Christmas. Derek Goodfellow, a senior District Commissioner between appointments, was sent to conduct him around the Province which he knew extremely well. So it was that my brother and I were attached, on a few occasions, to the great man's train as he progressed around Kasama District viewing deserving projects.

My father also toured, but I think only once, across a corner of Lake Tanganyika from Abercorn as it was then called (now Mbala). I believe my mother had been ill and she remained in camp in Abercorn, near civilisation, and because my sister and brother were to remain with her, Joey the cook also stayed behind. My mother usually prepared my father's touring box with the stores that he would need and which Joey would cook for him. On this occasion I was to cook for my father and it therefore seemed sensible for me to buy what was necessary from the Indian stores for the five days that we were to be away. I purchased, I thought with considerable intelligence, five tins of the large pork sausages that I recognised my mother occasionally served and of which I was inordinately fond. Five large tins of baked beans, a small sack of potatoes and a crate of beer completed my purchases. Not only, I reasoned, was the food tasty but I required the minimum of utensils to cook it and, even more important, it was within the scope of my culinary expertise. The first evening out after a hard day cycling round his schools, I duly prepared the sausages, baked beans and mashed potato on a fire outside the village school in which we had set up camp, and my father congratulated me on the result. The second night he congratulated me, I detected, with rather less enthusiasm. The third night he enquired, I thought in a rather marked fashion, if there was to be anything else on the menu. For the remaining nights he remained silent.

It was towards the end of the holiday that we did a day trip with my father to a place called Luingu, I think, where we spent the day with the District Commissioner, a stocky dynamic character called Jack Fairhurst, an old friend of my father's. As we travelled round with him and I watched what he had to do and how he did it and the way he interacted with the people we met, it suddenly came to me that this was what I wanted to do. I knew it was a hard life, often uncomfortable, sometimes dangerous, and not very well-paid (I guessed) but fascinating and rewarding. I reckoned that if the work was sufficiently demanding to keep someone like Jack Fairhurst interested and at full stretch, it must be worth trying.

With some trepidation I broke it to my parents that my plan to be a barrister had changed, or at least been put on hold, and that instead I proposed to follow his example and join the Colonial Service, not in education but in the Provincial Administration. Neither my father nor Len Bean, whose advice he sought and who kindly volunteered to give me a reference, tried to make me change my mind but they did warn me that the end of the expatriate Civil Service was already in sight. Indeed my father's next post which followed soon after our return to England was as Under-Secretary of State for Training to set up the first

Staff Training College and University to bring on young Africans to man the Civil Service. They had no idea as they spoke just how soon Macmillan's famous 'Wind of Change' speech would presage African Independence. At the same time as my father was promoted and transferred to Lusaka, Len Bean was appointed Secretary of State for Native Affairs and as such the Head of the Provincial Administration.

At the end of the holiday my sister and I flew back together. We broke our journey in Nairobi, as usual, where we stayed with the Attorney General, who was much in the news as a result of his prosecution of the Mau Mau leaders. As a result of this connection the Society section of the local paper reported our departure to England. 'Mr Goddard, who has been staying with the Attorney General and his wife, left this morning for London with his daughter.' The family were much amused.

CHAPTER 2

# Taking off

IN THE SUMMER OF 1961 I completed my degree course at Oxford,
became engaged to be married, and rowed for the second year in the
Head of the River crew and for the last time at Henley. Although the
college was not successful at Henley, it was a most enjoyable interlude.
We camped, most comfortably, in the garage of the lovely house of a
local doctor and dined every night at Phyllis Court for a ridiculously
discounted sum. The weather was wonderful and our rowing went well.
Our final coach as in the previous year was a London solicitor with the
most fabulous mansion set in acres of beautifully-manicured lawns on the
banks of the Thames. Our crew and the Jesus College crew from
Cambridge, which he also coached, were invited on the evening of the
Saturday before the Regatta, following our final dress rehearsal, to a
'modest' celebratory drink at his house. It was hinted to us and to the
Cambridge crew that the rig of the day ought to be the full uniform of
college blazer, tie and cap, white trousers and suede shoes and, of course,
(as we were all members of Leander) pink socks. In exchange for this
sartorial glory we were rewarded with apparently unlimited quantities of
champagne and strawberries and cream and the company of a host of
amazingly pretty girls that he had thoughtfully recruited for the occasion.

I had been offered permanent and pensionable employment as a
District Officer in the Colony of Northern Rhodesia, subject to a
satisfactory attendance for one year at the Overseas Services Course at
Cambridge and a two-year probationary period in Northern Rhodesia,
during which period I would be a District Officer Cadet at a starting
salary of £1,080 per annum. This offer followed a formal interview at
the Colonial Office in London, a daunting experience for even the most
brave-hearted. It had not been an unmitigated success. It followed what
I understand is the usual civil service format of a board of six or seven
eminent gentlemen (no women, of course), all no doubt with a different
expertise, sitting at a long table. I entered and was invited most kindly
to sit in the middle of another table which made a T with the table at
which the board were seated. Each member of the board was introduced,
although I do not imagine I could have remembered a single name even

five minutes later. Having got through the details of my education and upbringing the board gave me a grilling on my expectations of the length of my career in the Colonial Service, which, in view of the warnings of my father and his colleagues in Northern Rhodesia, was not easy. Eventually the chairman had the courtesy to explain that their questioning had been prompted by a letter, succulent pieces of which he read out, from one of my referees. My referee had taken the opportunity to express, in very forthright terms, his views on the likelihood of the whole Empire going to the dogs in the very near future and suggesting that it could be viewed as fraud to offer employment in a service that was on the verge of extinction. The board looked very dubious, despite my protestations that his views were not mine but fortunately the next question was to enquire what I proposed to do for mental relaxation in the long summer evenings when I was not engaged in my duties. In a flash of inspiration I answered that I had long been an admirer of T.S. Eliot (which was true) and that I fancied writing a play on the lines of his *Cocktail Party* which included, I reminded the board, a Chorus which appeared from time to time to comment on the action. I suggested that this might very easily translate to the typical outstation club and a Chorus of drinkers. Those members of the board who had experience of life in the Colonies were intrigued by this idea and thereafter, despite the attempts of the chairman to keep them in order, kept interrupting to suggest ideas for my proposed play.

This was at the end of June. I was due to start my Overseas Services Course at Cambridge in the September. My parents were overseas and unfortunately my flatmates had moved on to pastures new so I could not continue in the flat which we had shared most happily during our last year at university. I found instead a room just opposite the Casualty department of the Radcliffe Infirmary for a suspiciously low rent. The reason for the moderate rent was quickly explained by the appalling clamour of the ambulance bells in the early hours of every morning! Fortunately my future mother-in-law insisted that I should come and live at her charming cottage just outside Oxford. I had one final and unpleasant passage of arms with the landlady, an elderly lady whom I never saw in any garb other than a black overcoat and a black boater. She kept budgerigars in a cage but she had the unnerving habit, in the course of conversation, of unlatching the cage and allowing the budgerigars out. They would circle around the room alighting from time to time on the landlady's black straw hat. In moments of stress she would shake her head, dislodging the budgerigars and causing them to fly around, creating the unpleasant impression that she was launching the birds, like kamikazes, at one's head.

Very shortly after moving my kit into my new home I set off to Dorset, to work on a farm, returning to Oxford I suppose at the end of August. Although my future mother-in-law was happy to have me to stay, clearly I had to generate some income until the course started in Cambridge in October. Happily I noticed that they were in the process of building a new Law Library in Oxford and so I went along and volunteered my services for this worthwhile project. It is always difficult to be a 'new boy' and I felt very out of my depth when I presented myself at the site for the first day's work and was issued with a shovel and pointed towards a massive mound of rubble in a corner that the machine could not get at and told to load a dumper. The site seemed to have a lot of these corners. There were no introductions and I spent any time that I was not shovelling standing on my own while the rest of the gang, a mixture of full-timers fiercely loyal to the company, which coincidentally was based in Cambridge, and local part-timers, gossiped among themselves, studiously avoiding me although, from the glances in my direction, it was obvious that I was often the subject of their conversation.

The first two or three days were lonely and very hard work. Two things then happened which entirely changed the situation. Firstly, and most importantly, Danny appeared. Danny, weather-beaten and wiry, of medium height with terrible teeth and an engaging grin, was the archetypal Irishman. From the enthusiasm with which he was greeted it was obvious that he was a great favourite and even management was prepared to overlook his taking a day or so off when it suited him. At the first break it was clear from the looks in my direction that my arrival had been drawn to Danny's attention. He came straight over.

'They says you're a college boy?'

'Yes.'

'What did you study, sorr?'

'Law.'

Danny considered this. The others had drifted nearer to listen to his cross-examination.

'If you studied law you will know the difference between larceny of a dwelling and burglary then, sorr?'

'Larceny of a dwelling is committed during the day and burglary is the same thing committed after 6 p.m. and before 6 a.m.'

'Quite roight, sorr.'

And turning to his listeners he explained that that was exactly how the Judge had explained it following a recent appearance of a friend of his before the Court. The ice was broken and the others crowded closer to introduce themselves.

The second equally welcome development, a day or so later, was the non-arrival for work of the driver of one of the two dumpers. He was a strange little Irishman who was obviously mentally deficient. I could not understand why the others were so patient with him and did not subject him to the teasing that the other men were subjected to for much less excuse. The explanation was that the little man had a terrible temper that made it dangerous to interfere with him and the reason for his non-appearance, which was apparently likely to be permanent, was due to someone off-site not being aware of that danger. After an hour or so I suggested diffidently that someone ought to drive the dumper. There were no takers. Apparently driving a dumper was semi-skilled work which my colleagues (other than Danny who drove the other dumper) felt unqualified to undertake and they were amazed and grateful when I volunteered to do so. Thereafter I spent a happy six weeks bouncing around the site on my dumper being greeted with a smile or a joke by the men who always seemed to have time for a chat and a smoke. I became particularly fond of Danny who moved around the country with his wife in their luxurious caravan, keeping one step ahead of a string of affiliation orders (for Danny was very popular with the ladies). The irony was that Danny could not get his wife pregnant. He was an intelligent man and I remember chatting to him about the legal profession and his volunteering with great prescience that there were certain situations for which the Law did not always have an answer and that if I ever found myself with that kind of situation I should feel free to call upon Danny and his friends. I did indeed much later find the occasional situation when I would have been very tempted to call upon Danny and 'his friends'.

There was a jocular sequel to my time on the building site. In the October I went on to Cambridge for the twelve-month Overseas Services Course. This included learning the rudiments of *Chi Bemba* (one of the most widely used of the Northern Rhodesian languages), which was taught by a charming retired missionary. If, during the summer, the weather was good, it was his habit to take the small groups, into which he divided us for practical conversation, out in a punt, which I suppose eased the pain for him of listening to us fumbling with the language. And so it was one hot and lazy afternoon that I was lolling complete with boater on my head in a punt with my colleagues idly putting together unlikely conversational gambits in *Chi Bemba* when I became aware that a man, whom I had noticed had been operating a huge digger on the bank apparently excavating a new channel, was trying to attract my attention. 'Tony, you lazy bugger, don't you remember me?' Of course I did; it was Danny. I had forgotten that the company for whom we had worked had its base in Cambridge.

It was a novel experience to start as a new boy at a different university but with the important distinction that, with my degree from Oxford under my belt, I qualified as a graduate and was, as such, entitled to some additional consideration and allowed to wear a graduate gown rather than the undergraduate version. In practice I cannot recall any other advantages of my exalted status and in particular the 'in before midnight' rule still applied. However, as I was housed in an annexe to the college, and the only thing that prevented me coming in through my window at night was a screw that in theory prevented the window being lifted high enough to allow anyone to get in and out and, as I was in those days slim enough to squeeze through it, the rule was not much of a handicap.

I was particularly fortunate in that the college chosen for me for the year during which I was to attend the Overseas Services Course was Peterhouse. Peterhouse, like Teddy Hall, was a small friendly college. Unlike Teddy Hall, however, it appeared to be well endowed. More accurately, the kitchen was well endowed, apparently by some past foreign member of the college who, one imagines, was so appalled by the typical food and service that he gave a vast sum of money with the strict instruction that it should be used solely for the improvement of the kitchen and dining room. Whatever the truth of the story, the happy fact was that the food was excellent and was served in a marvellous dining hall by smart waiters in crisp white jackets. This was in contrast to the food at Teddy Hall which in my time (it has now enormously improved) was not distinguished and those serving it tended to be old ladies with surgical stockings. Every now and then it appeared that the kitchen at Peterhouse accumulated so much unspent money that it had to get rid of it, with the happy result that they would invent a special occasion so as to have an excuse for putting on a particularly sumptuous meal. In any event I had no difficult in integrating into the College after it was discovered that I was an oarsman and I was recruited as coach to the First Eight.

I imagine the Overseas Services Course must have passed into history very soon after my time. It was already an anachronism, as the colonies which we were being trained to administer became independent and recruited their own people to take over from us. As a relic of its history the course boasted its own very handsome administrative base in the middle of Cambridge, which included a comfortable club complete with bar and dining room, to which we could invite guests. It was a regular event for senior officers when on leave to call in to the club, whose excellent facilities they had enjoyed in their young days, and also to take the opportunity to meet the new intake. So it was that Derek Goodfellow who, by one of those turns of the wheel of fate, reappeared in my life as the new Provincial Commissioner of the Eastern Province, to which I had heard I was to be posted, sent word that he would be in Cambridge and would expect me to have lunch with him at the club. At the appointed hour he duly appeared. He was a striking figure – well over six foot with a fierce bottle-brush moustache and one arm. Although the bar was crowded there was a hush as he made his appearance and I made haste to go forward to greet him and to offer him a drink. As I turned towards the bar to collect his drink he called after me as to whether 'the Books' were still in their usual place. Without waiting for a reply he strode across to where there was a stack of leather-bound volumes containing formal group photographs of all of the courses, going back before the First World War. The hush continued as, one-handed, he leafed through the books until he came to an old photograph which appeared to afford him some considerable amusement. I returned with his drink. 'Tubby Fotheringay.' He pointed at a young man in the photograph. 'Went to Fiji and got eaten by the natives. Bloody funny!'

The ice being broken I made haste to introduce him to the crowd of young men, including by this time several young Africans from Northern Rhodesia, who had been recruited to join the Provincial Administration and were, like me, waiting with some impatience for the course to end so that they could get started on their careers.

The policy of 'Africanisation' as it was called was not universally welcomed, inevitable and appropriate though it was, and I recall a less pleasant occasion when another very senior officer on leave called to visit us and saw fit to chide me that he heard that my father was 'organising crash courses for Africans to take over from us.' Flushed with injured family pride, I replied that the crash courses my father was having to organise 'were due to the lack of foresight of senior officers of the Provincial Administration over the past twenty years.' It was his turn to go pink. To his credit it must be said that he immediately retracted his remark and apologised that it was inappropriate.

The course did eventually end. I rowed, unintentionally, in the Peterhouse First Eight when their stroke broke something the weekend before the start of Summer Eights and I was prevailed upon to take his place. It was of course Bumps racing, which meant that for each of the four nights of the races the boats from the colleges lined up one behind the other with a boat's length between them and when the signal was given each crew tried literally to bump the boat in front before the boat behind bumped it. The Cambridge course is nearly four times as long as the Oxford course, twenty minutes as opposed to five minutes, and so if either the boat behind did not catch your boat or you could not catch the boat in front you had a long row over. As stroke I had the right to set the pace and for the first two nights we set off at such a pace that each night we bumped the boat in front before they had got into their stride. On the third and fourth nights, however, the crew in front was made of sterner stuff and we found ourselves, after our initial sprint, forced to settle down and row the whole course which, unfit as I was, was for me an exhausting business.

My father had insisted that although I was to enter the Colonial Service I should nonetheless keep up my legal studies. During my time at Oxford I had enrolled at Grays's Inn as a first step towards becoming a barrister and embarked on that most extraordinary of all eccentric procedures in a profession noted for its eccentricity of 'eating my dinners' (a relic of the mediaeval system of apprenticeship). Sometimes I did this in company with my father who had been a student at Gray's for something like twenty years. Whenever he came home on leave he would eat some more dinners, promising himself that when he no longer had sons at Oxford and a daughter at Wycombe Abbey to support he could retire and pass the Bar Exams. Alas, dear man, he died in harness and never achieved his ambition to be called to the Bar.

I also took some preliminary Bar Exams. I had an exemption from most of the papers as a result of my work for my Law degree but there were a few that I had to pass to complete Part One of the Bar Exams. I mention this because not only did I pass these two or three papers but actually obtained a Distinction in one of them, my one and only academic distinction. I was amazed, but this was nothing compared to my father, who looked at me for some time as if he had been nurturing a foundling.

Soon after the end of term I married and after a brief honeymoon in Wales and a final day at Henley, as a spectator for a change, and an evening at the theatre to see Noel Coward's timely musical *Sail Away*, my young bride and I sailed away from Southampton on the *Transvaal Castle*, with most of my friends from the Cambridge course, en route for Northern Rhodesia.

It took us three days to travel by train from Cape Town to Lusaka where we stayed in the Government rest house while awaiting transfer, in our case by air, to our stations. Here we were taken under the wing of Nan Bean who, in the absence of my mother who was still in England on leave, kindly took it upon herself to do what was necessary to prepare us for life on an outstation. Top of the list came a paraffin refrigerator, a monstrous beast, that followed us with all our other household goods by CARS (Central African Road Services) lorry a week or so later. This refrigerator (it spurns the diminutive 'fridge') cost £100, an enormous sum compared to my annual starting salary of £1,080. Happily the Government allowed a loan for the purchase of refrigerators and, of course, life without it in the tropics would have been quite impossible. In due course we flew up to Fort Jameson, the Provincial capital of the Eastern Province.

This is perhaps an appropriate moment to say a few words about the background to my situation. Northern Rhodesia was in the process of moving from being a colony within the Central African Federation, ruled directly by the English Colonial office in London with a Governor representing the Crown, to a fully Independent Republic of which Kenneth Kaunda was to be the first president. My time in the country coincided with the uncomfortable intermediate period following the Monckton Commission Report and Harold Macmillan's 'wind of change' speech. The country continued to be run by European civil servants, such as my father, and their juniors, such as myself, under the English Crown, as represented by the Governor. Under an interim Constitution, however, there was a Legislative Council, partly elected and partly selected. The situation was thoroughly unsatisfactory and there was considerable political ferment in the country as the African population, under the leadership of Kaunda and his United National Independence Party and his rival Nkumbula and his National Party, pressed for full independence sooner rather than later.

In the provinces, however, government went on very much as it had always done. I said earlier that there was direct rule from London and although that was entirely correct the theory was that our rule was indirect through the existing institutions, namely the tribal Chiefs and their Councillors (who confusingly were called Assessors).On to this system was grafted an English-type local government system so that the Chiefs took the place of elected local government Councillors. The local

*England's Finest. District Officer Cadets on their way to Northern Rhodesia. The author is looking thoughtful with the hammer.*

government officers, who actually ran the local government departments in the tribal area (usually relatives of one or other of the Chiefs)
were, to add to the confusion, called Councillors. They operated
rudimentary departments on English lines: Administration, Treasury,
Roads etc. The Councillors were usually literate in English. The Chiefs
usually were not.

In addition to their local government function, which in practice was
more or less entirely delegated to the Councillors, the Chiefs were also
responsible for law and order and the administration of justice in their
areas. For the purpose of keeping law and order the Government paid
for two or three *kapassus*, depending on the size of their populations
(*kapassu* being sufficiently translated for our present purposes as village
Policeman). For the administration of Justice the Government paid for
two Assessors, learned in tribal law, to sit with and advise the Chiefs
when they sat in judgement. They were also provided with a Court
Clerk, who, unlike the Assessors, was literate, although not necessarily in
English, so that they could keep a written note of the facts of the cases
that appeared before the Chiefs and of the Chiefs' decisions.The
authority of the Crown vested in the Governor, cascaded down, as it
were, through the Provincial Commissioners and District Commissioners
to the District Officers and eventually to such a lowly functionary as
District Officer Cadet Goddard.

Our department was known as the Provincial Administration (usually
shortened to the PA) and we, its officers, were responsible in effect for
'government' in our various areas, working through, and preferably with,
the tribal Chiefs. In that role we were assisted by the technical
departments such as Agriculture, Health, Public Works (roads and
buildings) and the like, and, of course, the Police. In our areas, working
through our tribal Chiefs, we were responsible for ensuring that the local
authority organization was operating satisfactorily. We were also responsible for supervising the Chiefs' courts, which entailed ensuring that case
records were produced and reading at least a proportion of them. So far
as law and order was concerned (and in my time this was a major
preoccupation of both the Chiefs and of the District Officers) our role
was to remind the Chiefs of their responsibilities to uphold the law in
their areas and thereafter to act in support of any action they might take.
For this purpose we might employ our Messengers or if necessary by
calling in the Police. The Chiefs were, often most reluctantly, very much
in the front line, being under pressure from the political parties to
cooperate with them against each other and on occasions the Govern-

ment and at the same time under pressure from the District Officers to take a strong line with the political parties if they stepped out of line.

In flagrant breach of the doctrine of the separation of powers, the officers of the Provincial Administration also exercised a judicial function. They were responsible for examining the court records of the Chiefs' courts (which were mainly concerned with family cases) with the power, in the case of senior officers, to call in for review cases that attracted their attention. They also acted as court of appeal for any cases in which one of the parties had the temerity to risk the ire of the Chief by appealing his decision. These functions were probably unexceptional but in addition the senior officers such as District Commissioners and District Officers with the necessary years' service also acted in effect as Stipendiary Magistrates, dealing with local crime and notwithstanding that on outstations they often operated as Policemen, particularly in cases of civil disturbance. By my time this difficulty was largely avoided by the increasing appointment of lawyers to sit as Resident Magistrates in the provincial headquarters to whom hard-pressed District Commissioners were only too pleased to remit their criminal cases.

Fort Jameson was both a provincial and district capital so that it boasted not only a Provincial Commissioner and his staff but also a District Commissioner and his District Officers and staff. The technical departments replicated this arrangement. There were three districts within the province: Fort Jameson, Lundazi to the north and Petauke to the south, on the road to the capital Lusaka and known, for its importance if not for its quality, as the Great East Road. There were also two sub-stations – Katete and Chadiza, which were staffed by senior District Officers rather than by full District Commissioners. There were three tribes in the Fort Jameson district – the *Chewa*, the *Ngoni* and, furthest from the town in the Luangwa valley, was the smallest of the three tribes, the *Kunda*.

The headquarters of the Provincial Administration in an area was always known as the *boma* (literally thorn fence thrown up by the early District Officers to keep the lions out). This name was capable of considerable extension so that it would apply to my (grass not thorn) fence thrown up on tour. It would also apply to the town of Fort Jameson where the headquarters of the Provincial Administration in the district was situated. Within the town of Fort Jameson it was the name given to the offices of the Provincial Administration. I use the word in all three senses.

The most striking feature of every *boma* was the platoon of Messengers in their starched blue bush jackets with red facings and blue shorts. A black bush hat, army boots and long puttees completed their uniform. There were approximately thirty-five of them at Fort Jameson and I imagine the same applied to most *bomas*. The District Commissioner always complained that there were never enough. Their title of 'Messenger' is entirely misleading as to their real function. They were accorded the dignity of their own piece of legislation which appointed them to be 'the eyes and ears' of the Government and they were indeed that but much, much more. Where, as in the Eastern Province, there was a history of military service, it was common for retired soldiers to be recruited as Messengers, but clearly the recruiting authority (I suppose the District Commissioner and the Senior Messenger) thought it necessary to keep a balance between civilian and ex-Askari recruits to prevent the force becoming too militaristic.

They certainly had to be brave and self-confident and they undoubtedly and very properly regarded themselves as an elite corps but braggarts were discouraged. District Officers always had at least one Messenger with them whenever they were on government business and probably three or four when out on tour away from the *boma* for any length of time. They also operated on their own or in pairs out in the villages acting as 'the eyes and ears of the Government' and with their distinctive uniforms were a very obvious support of the Chiefs' *kapassus*. They had a Policeman's power of arrest and like a Policeman carried a whistle, a pair of handcuffs and a short truncheon. Otherwise they were unarmed. All Messengers spoke some English and some good English. There is no doubt that the Messengers were the backbone of the English administration of Northern Rhodesia. They also on occasions did carry messages, travelling miles on their bicycles.

A few weeks after my arrival in Fort Jimmy, I found myself on my own, on my twenty-third birthday, attending a meeting in Chief Nsefu's village. I was feeling very lonely. As an unexpected addition to the purpose of the meeting it was reported that a villager had been found hanging by his neck from a branch at the very top of a very tall tree. 'How very fortunate' the cry went up 'that our new District Officer is here to tell us what to do.' It sounded like a genuine suicide but would someone who wanted to take his own life really go to the trouble of climbing to the very top of an extremely tall and, as I saw for myself, difficult-to-climb tree to carry out his dire intent. And then again the Kunda had a reputation for guile equalled only by their reputation for doing away with unwanted neighbours. An inquest was clearly called for but who performed the function of Coroner and what was the procedure? The answer to the 'who?' question was undoubtedly 'the District Officer' but did I, as a very new cadet, count as a District Officer for this purpose? And I had not a clue as to the procedure to be adopted. It was as I gazed out across the heads of the expectant crowd looking for inspiration that I saw the already familiar blue and red uniform. The Messenger dismounted at the edge of the crowd, leaned his bicycle against a convenient tree and after a pat at his dusty uniform, marched smartly along the lane that had been made in the crowd and came to a halt in front of the table, which as usual, had been placed before me as a desk. He saluted and took two more steps closer to the table where he halted again and then, to the count of one-two, one-two, placed his hand on the message pouch attached to his belt and produced two envelopes which he handed to me. He saluted again and waited for me to read the messages that he had cycled 100 miles on his own over execrable roads in the heat to deliver. One was a reminder about an outstanding account from Henley Regatta and the other was a birthday card from my parents. 'No reply,' I said. 'Will you stop for a rest and a meal and travel back by Land-Rover tomorrow?'

'No,' he replied, explaining that if he started back now and stopped the night on the road and left early the next morning he would be back at the *boma* before me.

When a Messenger was not out on tour he remained at the *boma* where, after a daily inspection by the District Commissioner and some drill directed by the Senior Messenger, he was free to sit and gossip with his colleagues in the shade unless called to run some errand or attend to some duty. All, that is, except for the Senior Messengers, who were allocated to one or other of the District Officers, and who had the duty of sitting outside the office of their own District Officer, or District Officer Cadet in my case. This had the disadvantage that he or his deputy would leap to his feet and crash to attention whenever the District Officer left or returned to his office. It did, however, have the advantage of warning of the approach of senior officers (every one was senior to me) to whom they rendered the same honour if ever they passed by.

And the body in the tree? Oh, I appointed myself unofficial Coroner, certified that there were no suspicious circumstances and ordered that the body be taken down and buried. Even if enquiries had been made no one would ever have got at the truth of the matter, I reassured myself.

We flew up to Fort Jameson with Jim, one of the other cadets from the Cambridge Course who had travelled out ahead of his fiancée, who joined him later. Jim was a martial arts enthusiast who had persuaded the

majority of those on the Overseas Services Course to subscribe to the
hire of a Japanese grand master to teach us the rudiments of *Aikido*, a
fiendish Japanese (or was it Korean?) method of self-defence, which
involved doing unpleasant things to one's assailant's joints. As far as I
know none of us ever had to resort to using the Art in earnest, but I am
sure that, had we had to do so, we would have given a good account of
ourselves. Jim and I had been told in England not only that we had both
been posted to the Eastern Province but it had even been hinted that Jim
was to go as Officer in Charge of the Kunda Valley Native Authority
and its chiefs and I was to go as second-in-command to Chadiza.

Our first port of call in Fort Jimmy was the *boma* to report to the
District and Provincial Commissioners. We started with the Provincial
Commissioner who, in a bush jacket, shorts and long socks, looked far
more at home than he had at the Overseas Services Club in Cambridge.
He began by telling us what we already knew, namely that there were
two posts on offer, one in the Kunda valley and the other in Chadiza and
went on to enquire whether we had decided between ourselves who was
to go where, as it did not matter to him how we allocated ourselves
although, if we could not make up our minds, he would make the
decision for us. We were both rather non-plussed by this and seeing our
hesitation the Provincial Commissioner suggested that we toss for it. We
both agreed. He produced a coin which he spun for us. I got the Kunda
valley and Jim Chadiza. We were, I think, both pleased with the way
things turned out.

Fort Jimmy was a pleasant town attractively situated in a hollow in the
Chipata hills. The offices of the various Government departments were
sited in the middle of the town around the *boma*. The bungalows for the
senior civil servants, in practice at that time entirely European, were set
in tree-lined roads on the lower slopes of one of the hills conveniently
close to the golf course (with sand greens). There was a substantial
African township, known as Chipata, which subsequently at independence gave its name to the whole town, Fort Jameson being regarded,
no doubt, as politically incorrect by the new administration. This
township was largely populated by African employees of the Government of one type or another. There was an airport with a grass runway,
an African and a European hospital (set some way apart from each other),
and a club called the Victorian Memorial Institute where there were a
well-patronised bar and some tennis courts, in our time restricted, in
practice if not in theory, to Europeans. Fort Jimmy was older than most
of the towns in Northern Rhodesia having been founded towards the end

of the Cecil Rhodes era by one of his lieutenants, Leander Jameson. Unusually, there was still a small, but significant number of while settlers with farms and businesses in the area. The venerability of the club building and the Anglican Church (the latter built as exact a reproduction of an English country church as dried bricks would allow) reflected this. There was also a magnificent modern Roman Catholic Cathedral at the White Fathers' mission on the outskirts of the town. There were some Indian stores and a big Indian community. These stores attempted, not always successfully, to cater for the wants of both the African and European communities. A visit, to Mr Deya's emporium for instance, tended to be frustrating. He would greet one with the assurance that 'Every ting we gottings.' Unhappily a request for even the most mundane item was all too often greeted with a shake of the head 'that we not gottings but every ting else we gottings' and so on for everything else one wanted.

We were sorry to see Jim disappear off to Chadiza leaving us to settle into what was, to begin with, a very new and often daunting 'grown-up' environment. We lived for weeks in the Government Guest House (a rudimentary kind of hotel, under the supervision of the District Commissioner, for those newly arrived or making a brief visit) while our new bungalow was made ready for us. This meant that our main baggage, which soon arrived, had to go into store, entailing irritating visits to the store to try to retrieve items that were needed and to remember in which trunk they had been packed. As a fully qualified secretary my wife very quickly obtained employment with the Education Department, leaving me to learn my trade as a District Officer.

My immediate superior was a very senior District Commissioner who, although possessing great charm, gave the appearance of being constantly under pressure, which he probably was. He had recently remarried and had a young family and the, by now, obvious signs that the future of the European administration was coming to an end, must have been a worry to him. It must also have been difficult to serve under, and have an office just next door to that of, the charismatic but irascible Provincial Commissioner. The stories about the Provincial Commissioner were legion; my favourite dates back to his early days as a District Officer in charge of an outstation. His supervising District Commissioner was out on tour on the edge of the outstation district and decided it would be discourteous, being so close, not to drop in, albeit without warning. Arriving at the *boma* he was surprised not to see any of the Messengers in their distinctive uniforms, who were such a feature of every *boma*.

Mystified, he called out and after a few shouts was rewarded by a call from a nearby clump of tall trees. He went over to investigate and to his amazement found a small army of Messengers roosting in the higher branches of the trees. 'Come down at once and explain what you are doing,' he shouted.

'No,' they called back, they couldn't do that. The Bwana Goodfellow was away on tour for the day and he had told them they were to stay in the trees until he got back. They were too fearful of what the Bwana District Officer would do if they disobeyed him to come down even for the District Commissioner. They went on to explain that Bwana Goodfellow had told them (for reasons they were reluctant to admit) that if they 'wanted to behave like bloody monkeys they would bloody well live like bloody monkeys for a day.'

Looking back, this kind of behaviour sounds, and no doubt was, monstrous but from my own observation I can vouch for the fact that the Africans not only respected but were genuinely fond of him. Certainly his bluff manner hid a very soft heart for children, young District Officers and village Africans, all of whom he treated in exactly the same way. Whether he was the right man to deal with the prickly educated and semi-educated political leaders who were now prolific in the area was another matter.

The *boma* in Fort Jimmy was a pleasant single-storey building in the form of an E, with the central prong replaced with an entrance passageway giving on to a covered veranda running along the 'inside' of the building. The district administrative offices occupied the whole of the main building. The Provincial Commissioner's offices were con-tained in a much smaller office-block behind the main building and directly in line with the central entrance. The central entrance and both of the wings of the building were finished with Dutch-style facades with scalloped edges. The whole was set (thanks to the local prison population) in well-manicured lawns. Despite the verandas and fans, the offices were horrendously hot particularly in the summer and we started at 7.30 in the morning so as to be able to finish at 1.30 in the afternoon.

The District Commissioner was supported by two experienced District Officers being appointed, one to supervise the Ngoni Native Authority and the other the Chewa Native Authority and their respective chiefs. The third tribe, the Kunda, being much smaller (24,000 people) merited, if it merited a District Officer of its own at all, a less senior officer, in my case a District Officer Cadet.

*Fort Jimmy boma during the Governor's visit.*

There were, I believe, European secretaries and at least one European District Assistant and Accountant on the staffs of both the Provincial and District Commissioners. In mitigation of my lack of recollection of my colleagues I plead that as soon as I became properly installed as District Officer Kunda I spent most of my time on tour and very little time in the office. My first few days were spent reading uncomprehendingly through the huge untidy Kunda files that the District Commissioner directed should be brought to me from the Central Registry, the laudable theory being the hope that I might learn something of what was happening in the area for which I was about to become responsible under his supervision. He had intended, I have no doubt, to keep a close eye on my activities but he was so preoccupied by the serious political unrest that was brewing, particularly in Fort Jameson township, that he had perforce largely to leave me to my own devices. The Provincial Commissioner had been more forthright. 'I don't want to hear from you or about you for at least six months. If I do it will mean you either want to give me some advice, which you will not be qualified to do, or you will be in trouble, which I won't want to hear either.'

I was in any event grateful when, after some days' reading the files in the heat and unaccustomed confines of an office, the District Commissioner suggested that I might like to lead a tax drive that one of the senior Messengers was organising over the next few days. The tax regime was devastatingly simple in that every one, with virtually no exceptions, was required to pay a poll tax of some small sum every year and they were given a receipt to prove that they had paid. The poll tax presented no problems for those in employment but was a serious burden for subsistence farmers who formed the bulk of the rural population. The tax drive that was being mounted was around the fringes of the township where the majority of the population were in employment and could well afford the tax. But being away from their home villages and the headman who would put them under pressure to pay they considered, usually correctly, that they were unlikely to be caught. In any event I spent several busy and moderately productive days with a party of Messengers and a Senior Messenger sweeping through the villages and hamlets around the town and calling impromptu meetings to examine tax receipts and extract payment or promises of payment from defaulters.

On occasions our proceedings were enlivened by having to give chase to young men whose consciences clearly troubled them, and who had decided to rely on their fleetness of foot to avoid the necessity of discussing their tax situation with us. On a couple of occasions our quarry had escaped over a boundary fence into what I was told was a European farm where the Messengers were very reluctant to go. This rankled and on the next occasion someone tried to escape by disappearing over a fence, I called to the Messengers to follow me over the fence and onto the farm. Reassured by my promise that I would accept full responsibility, my team of Messengers enthusiastically followed me across some scrubland and into what was obviously the farm village which our quarry was even then entering. Deciding that I might as well be hung for a sheep as a lamb, I ordered that the entire population of the village should assemble with their tax receipts while we carried out a search for the young man we were following. Word had, however, obviously gone to the Big House and no sooner had I started to examine the tax receipts than the white farmer arrived in his Land-Rover in a veritable storm of dust. He was exquisitely polite. 'Was I aware that this was his property and he could not recall receiving notice to expect what appeared to be a punitive expedition from the provincial administration. As for tax, I had perhaps forgotten the arrangement he had with the District Commissioner, that in exchange for the inconvenience, on both sides, of having young men from the *boma* calling to collect the tax, he did the tax-collecting himself, by inviting a clerk from the *boma* to visit the farm each year so that he could ensure that everyone on his farm paid their tax.'

At this moment two of my Messengers appeared with the young man under close arrest. The farmer turned a dangerous shade of white under his tan. 'That is my foreman,' he said through gritted teeth. 'Of course he has paid his tax. Show them your tax receipt,' he said to the unhappy young man who, to my enormous relief, could only hang his head and admit that, unusually, this year he had not paid his tax. It seemed an appropriate moment to make my escape, and apologising for overlooking the arrangement the District Commissioner had negotiated, we made our escape. I heard nothing more of the incident and when I subsequently met the farmer socially he was perfectly pleasant and so obviously no grudges were held.

At the end of the week I was about to return to my files when another older and more senior cadet at the end of his first tour who had, as a temporary measure, been looking after the Kunda valley, was encouraged by the District Commissioner to give me a brief introduction to the valley. He was not, strictly, my 'predecessor' having only spent a few months as an interregnum in the Kunda area. He had been the first District Officer to spend even that amount of time solely in the Kunda

*Butterfly and chrysalis. District Officer Cadet Goddard and District Officer Ngoni at the Katete Show.*

valley for some years, it having usually been attached as an unwelcome accretion to the duties of District Officer Chewa. It was his report that things were getting out of control in the valley (which was dangerous in the light of the worsening political situation) that led to my appointment as the first full-time District Officer Kunda for some time.

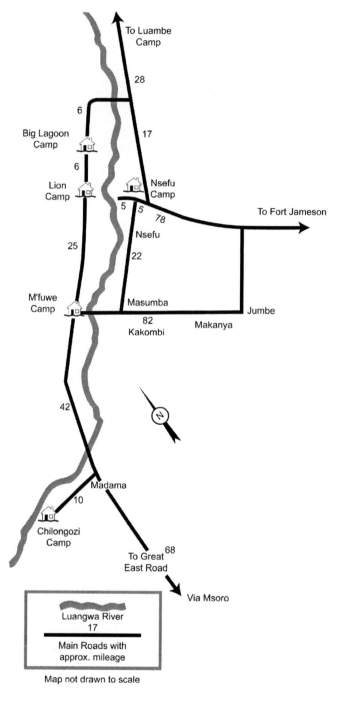

To Luambe
Camp

28

6

17

Big Lagoon
Camp

6

Lion
Camp

Nsefu
Camp

5  5

78

Nsefu

To Fort Jameson

25

22

M'fuwe
Camp

Masumba

Jumbe

82

Makanya

Kakombi

42

N

Madama

10

Chilongozi
Camp

To Great
East Road

68

Via Msoro

Luangwa River
17

Main Roads with
approx. mileage

Map not drawn to scale

*The Kunda Native Authority Area*

# CHAPTER 3

# The Kunda Valley

THE LUANGWA VALLEY ('the Valley' as it was always known) for which, aged twenty-three, I was to be responsible, ran from north to south between the Northern and the Eastern Provinces. The Luangwa River was the boundary between the two and it was therefore the western extremity of the Eastern Province. The Valley lay several hundred feet below the rest of the province being set in a rift valley, similar to the Great Rift Valley of East Africa, so that going to and from Fort Jimmy, which lay more or less in the middle of the province, one had to ascend or descend from the escarpment which lay between the Valley and the plateau on which Fort Jimmy was fortunate to be sited. There was a noticeable change in temperature as one descended into the Valley. It also formed a tsetse boundary between the Valley, which was inundated with tsetse flies whose bites were a constant irritation, and the plateau which, at least in theory, was free of the fly and therefore of sleeping sickness. Cattle were accordingly raised on the plateau and played an important part in the life of the Chewa and Ngoni tribes.

The Valley was indeed not a healthy place in which to operate. In addition to sleeping sickness which prohibited the keeping of cattle (game were not affected), its inhabitants also suffered, ironically in view of the heat, from chest troubles, including TB, and known whatever its manifestation as *chifua* (the cough). That was, of course, in addition to the usual perils of malaria and bilharzia and the other tropical horrors. I was also told that it was one of the breeding grounds of the plague known in Europe in the Middle Ages as the Black Death! It redounds to the credit of my young wife, a doctor's daughter, that neither of us ever suffered from the effects of any of these ills due, I am sure, to her insistence on good regular meals and a high degree of hygiene.

The Kunda tribe, for whom I was to be responsible, occupied the southern end of the Valley, the top of the Valley being in the adjoining Lundazi District. The Kunda were not a warrior tribe, being small in stature, which no doubt explained their tribal area being in an insalubrious valley, but they had a reputation as hunters and poisoners. The kindly, gentle paramount chief, Nsefu, was credited with a personal score in double figures. There were five other Kunda Chiefs: Jumbe, a rather fierce old man at the top of the Valley (nearest to Fort Jimmy), Mnkanya and Kakumbi in the middle of the Valley. Kakumbi's area finished at the river where there was a ferry across the river to the game camp of Norman Carr, who was very well-known as a game scout. Nsefu's large area adjoined Kakumbi and Mnkanya to the north and was also bounded to the west by the Luangwa River, although most of the area along the river had been dedicated by a previous chief as a game reserve. Nsefu's area occupied the north-western quadrant of the Kunda tribal area. The corresponding south-eastern quadrant, which was in hills set back some way from the river, was the domain of Chief Msoro, a reserved, thoughtful man who had the dubious privilege of acting as host to a large, old, established UMCA (Universities Mission to Central Africa) mission. The area between Msoro and the river was occupied by little Malama with six villages adjoining Chilangozi Game Reserve at the extreme south-western corner of the Kunda Valley.

The Kunda Valley was not over-endowed with roads (as opposed to the tracks which meandered between villages and which were sometimes passable by Land-Rover and sometimes not). The road into the Valley (compacted gravel and very corrugated) split as it reached the Valley, the lesser road going straight on to the west and Nsefu and the Nsefu Game Reserve. The main road turned nearly at right angles towards the south and to Chief Jumbe's capital, where the Kunda Native Authority offices were situated. After Jumbe (the town took its name from the chief) the road turned west again, through the areas of Chiefs Mnkanya and Kakumbi, towards the Luangwa where in effect it ended at Norman Carr's game camp. There was a minor road which branched south along the river to the Chilongozi Game Reserve and Chief Malama's villages. There was also a minor road to Chief Nsefu's area which branched off from the main road at a village called Masumba, which was the geographical centre of the Valley, distinguished by having a copse of enormous baobab trees. The road to Chief Msoro's area and the UMCA mission did not use the main Valley road at all but branched off on its own from the Great East Road some miles out of Fort Jameson. A kind of road continued beyond Msoro to Malama. There was alleged to be a track between Msoro and Jumbe. I have a distant memory of having tried it once, but it was to all intents and purposes impracticable except on foot.

The land itself was very varied. There were considerable areas of mopane woodland, many of the trees growing to a great height. There were also large areas of open grassland studded with small trees, particularly in the Nsefu area, and many areas where there was a mixture of the two, in other words open grassland dotted with occasional areas of substantial trees. The Agriculture Department assured me the Valley was potentially very productive but was not properly exploited by the locally-preferred policy of 'slash and burn'. Under this practice during the dry season the local population cut the tops off the trees and heaped them over the area intended as their gardens. They then burned the wood, which released potash and other minerals onto the soil into which they planted their sorghum or maize at the onset of the rains. The system required the minimum of effort and left the Kunda with the maximum of time for hunting and socialising. It did, however, require a small population in relation to the available land as it was necessary to move to new gardens every year to give the trees on which the practice depended several years to regenerate. The agricultural problems of the valley were a climate which encouraged lassitude, an amazing host of bugs and plant diseases and the depredations of the local elephant and baboon populations.

For my first brief introduction to the Valley I enjoyed the luxury of leaving it to my predecessor to make all the arrangements and I merely tagged along to learn the lie of the land. One of the advantages of Jumbe was a spacious brick-built Government rest house with four good-sized rooms set in pairs either side of a large central veranda where one could sit and eat and receive visitors in comparative cool. There was an outside kitchen. Because it was used only occasionally, and then only by Government officers with business in the Valley, it was not manned nor did it have the usual store of tins and supplies. There were, however, a few Indian stores half a mile away if one was short of supplies. It was here that I spent my first few nights in the valley with my predecessor, Bill. The next day we visited the modern and well-appointed Native Authority offices and I was introduced to the Councillors. The Administrative Councillor was a well-qualified outsider who acted as chief executive of the Authority. On his shoulders fell the responsibility for reconciling, or at least attempting to reconcile, the often competing demands of the Chiefs and the Government, as represented by the District Officer for the time being responsible for the Kunda. Increasingly he had to take into account the interests and demands of the local UNIP office holders. The treasurer was a son of Chief Jumbe. The Councillor responsible for health (in effect a few local clinics) was a *Chulu* (that is a member of the Paramount Chief's family). There were also Councillors in charge of Public Works and Agriculture but I cannot

now remember their family connections. There was a certain air of
'make-believe' about the whole operation. With a few exceptions the
calibre of the Councillors was pretty low and their appointment was,
more often than not, more a way of rewarding family membership than
a recognition of ability. To be fair the funds available to them did not
enable them to do very much and any major schemes originated and
were resourced by Central Government.

After this I was introduced to the ancient art of touring. My
predecessor had no time to do more than just show me what was
involved by taking me by bicycle on a circular tour around a few local
villages in Chief Jumbe's area. It was not an edifying exercise. The
villages we toured were, I hoped, not typical, scruffy, and sunk in a
hopeless torpor which made it apparently impossible for the villagers
(mainly old men and women and children) to do anything to improve
their miserable condition. I sat with increasing irritation while Bill went
through the motions, or so it seemed to me, of enquiring into the
situation of the villages we visited. On each visit he would introduce me
as the new District Officer, and then courteously ask if I had anything
to add to his final remarks, usually platitudes about keeping the village
clean and planting early so as to catch the rains. I had previously thanked
Bill for his invitation but declined to address the village, but at the final
village my frustration finally got the better of me and I accepted the
opportunity to say a few words. The village had the considerable
distinction of being the most loathsome of all that we had visited and the
headman the most arrogant. Speaking through the *boma* clerk, whom Bill
had brought along to interpret and keeping my voice quiet, I said all the
things I had been bottling up for the past two days. I told them that their
village was a disgrace, and I dilated with some fervour on the particulars
of the charge. I told the headman that he was largely to blame for the
state of the village and I promised to make sure that the Chief was made
aware of my displeasure and so on and so forth. The clerk, who had been
translating, entirely automatically, for Bill, glanced at Bill for reassurance
when he realised what he was being asked to translate. Bill just shrugged
It was a matter for me, his shrug implied, if I wanted to start my career
by offending my parishioners. Given this reassurance the clerk clearly
entered into the spirit of the occasion and by the startled and then
apprehensive looks appearing the faces of the headman and the village
elders my remarks lost nothing in the translation.

I would like to be able to report that when I returned to the village,
which I made a point of doing very soon, I found it transformed. It is

true that some cosmetic improvements had been made but in all essentials it remained as unlovely as I had originally found it. My outburst was, however, apparently widely reported and for some time, whenever I visited a village, it was obvious from the villagers' apprehensive expressions that they were expecting a repeat performance.

When I got back to the *boma*, I lost no time in organising to return to the Valley for which my few days' introduction with Bill had served only to whet my appetite. We were still in the Government rest house, which we were finding increasingly irksome. Our acquisition of our first retainer, Peter, solved the problem, we hoped, of who was to look after us on tour. There was no shortage of servants looking for positions, some with excellent references from previous officers for whom they had worked. Peter, a Bemba from the Northern Province, had, however, worked for my parents as a garden boy-cum-kitchen boy. He had lodged with my parents' long time cook, Joey, who had become very fond of him. When Peter heard that I was to come out to Africa and to the Eastern Province, he suggested to my parents that he should come to work for me as houseboy/cook. My parents endorsed his suggestion. As Joey (an Ngoni) was to be on leave in or near Fort Jimmy while my parents were on leave in England, he would be able to induct Peter into our employment and teach him the mysteries of European Cooking. My mother promised that she also would give him some coaching in the culinary skills before she left to go on leave. As we did not yet have a house, and therefore the servants' quarters that came with it, Peter had had to postpone his journey from the Northern to the Eastern Province and was now becoming restive to make a start in his new position which he regarded as promotion. It was accordingly agreed that although we still did not have a house (it was promised to be very nearly ready) he would travel to Fort Jimmy in order to come with us on tour and thereafter, if the house was still not ready, he would lodge with Joey and his wife at their house in Chipata township. I also suggested, and to my relief Joey agreed, that he would come on tour with us although in a purely supervisory capacity. My wife had not yet started as a secretary in the Education Department and so she was free to come as well.

The next step was to organise the tour. I approached the District Officer in charge of the Ngoni and asked him what to do.

'Tell your Messenger to lay it on. He'll know how to do it.'

'But which Messenger shall I ask?' I enquired.

'Your own Senior Messenger, of course.'

'But I haven't been given a Messenger.'

'Of course you have. The one who sits outside your door,' he reassured me. I had been exchanging greetings with the huge elderly Messenger with a wonderful face who did indeed seem to spend all his days sitting on a chair outside my office. I had assumed this was simply because his age and seniority entitled him to sit comfortably in the shade while his junior colleagues had less comfortable positions under the trees.

On my return to my office I stopped to introduce myself to this self-same Messenger who leaped to attention at my approach. Thus it was that Senior Messenger James Chirwa stamped into my life. For the next two years he was to be my constant companion, counsellor, protector and friend. He also on occasions drove me nearly hysterical with rage. On this first occasion, having exhausted my few words of *Chinyanja* greeting, I called a Clerk to interpret that I intended to go on tour to Chief Nsefu's area and that my wife would be coming with me. Could he organise this? Did we have to give notice to the Chief of our intended visit? How many days would we need to be away? What equipment would we need in the way of tents and beds? What about transport? James's face lit up. He obviously relished the idea of some old-fashioned touring of which, I gathered, there had been very little recently. We should certainly send a Messenger ahead to inform the Chief and the Native Authority of our intended tour and he would stay on to prepare for our arrival, including supervising the building of the grass *boma* in which we would camp, and recruit a few local labourers, who at Government expense, would cut wood and carry water for us throughout our stay, which he estimated would need to be some ten days if we were to tour the area properly. We would need a tent and mosquito nets and campbeds and folding tables, chairs and a canvas bath and washbasin, all of which would be provided by the *boma* out of its store. We would need a Land-Rover to take us and our and his personal effects and a flat-bed Bedford lorry to take everything else. And presumably he should organise to take one of the *boma* 14-bore shotguns for guinea fowl and a .303 for larger game? I would have to sign for these and obtain a 'pot licence' to authorise me to shoot 'for the pot' while on tour. I would also need to collect an imprest of small coins to pay our labour and to cover any other out-of-pocket expenses.

I expressed my reservations about the offensive weapons and explained that I had no experience of big game hunting or for that matter any kind of shooting. He expressed shock at my admission. It was absolutely de rigueur, he erroneously assured me, for a District Officer on tour to provide his followers with a regular supply of meat. Unconvinced, I

*Senior Messenger James Chirwa.*

reluctantly agreed to take the weapons and even obtained a 'pot' licence from the District Commissioner which entitled me to shoot an impressive range of game provided it was strictly for the consumption on tour of me and my staff.

'And how many servants would we be bringing to look after us?' James asked. I explained about Peter and it was his turn to look dubious. I hastened to explain that Joey would be coming with us and he brightened. Although James was of the Chewa tribe, he knew Joey as an old friend. Everyone seemed to know Joey, who had toured extensively with my father when my father was for some years the Provincial Education Officer of the Eastern Province.

A week or so later, and after some hectic searching through our boxes in store to find bed-linen and cooking pots and utensils and knives and forks, the great day dawned and we set off for the Valley. That, however, is to draw a veil over the trauma of packing into a Land-Rover and a lorry everything that we would need for ten days in the bush (the transport was to leave us and return to the *boma* until the date fixed for our return). On top of the tents and beds and other *boma* equipment and our own pots and pans and stores for ten days, we had to find space for ourselves, two drivers, James and three other Messengers, and their admittedly very modest belongings. This Herculean task was made infinitely worse by the vociferous pleas of a horde of women, all with huge bundles on their heads and children slung on their backs, to be given a lift to the Valley and all of whom had, by some strange coincidence, discovered a close relationship to one or other of the Messengers, usually James. They were reluctant to take 'No' for an answer and as fast as the drivers and I chased one heavily-loaded woman off one side, another, equally heavily-laden, would climb up on the other side.

These battles for transport were a regular feature of life in the Valley. There was a real need for people to get to and from Fort Jimmy and, within reason and the capability of the springs of my Land-Rover, I was happy to oblige. It was, however, one area where James and I did not see eye to eye and he was for ever trying to squeeze one extra woman with an impossibly large load and four children on to a Land-Rover that was very obviously already grossly overloaded. The usual plea was that she (or occasionally he) was a sister or brother, as indeed they probably were in terms of the African extended family, but it was seldom that he could confirm, in answer to my question about the relationship, 'same fazzer same muzzer' with a triumphant smile.

We eventually arrived in the Valley, having survived the road down the escarpment, and passed through the tsetse posts where, on the way out, we would have to stop and be searched for any flies that might be trying to hitch a lift in our vehicle or on our person. I came to find these posts, where we were required to enter in a book name, vehicle registration number and date and time, very useful for keeping an eye on the movements of the ungodly. In the late afternoon we arrived, hot, dusty and shaken, at Chief Nsefu's village. I had toured quite often with my father, both as a child and when I visited during my last vacation as an undergraduate, but usually we had stayed in rest houses and, when none was available, we had camped outside a village or occasionally inside a school. Nothing had prepared me for the honour that was done to even such an insignificant ornament of the Provincial Administration as myself.

The villagers, under orders from the Chief and the supervision of the Messenger that James had sent on ahead, had erected an elephant grass fence standing some six to eight-foot high, enclosing the best part of half an acre. Inside this enclosure had been erected several huts for stores and kitchen and a larger one with half bamboo walls to serve as an office. Set some way away were two small grass enclosures, one to serve as a bathroom (in which the canvas bath and washbasin from the *boma* would be put) and the other, for an equally obvious purpose, had a very large pit partly covered by wooden branches, above which an ingenious seat made of grass had been woven. On this the wooden loo seat brought from the *boma* would be placed. On a later occasion, when my mother-in-law came on tour with us while she was on a visit, I observed James and the senior labourer deep in conversation as they followed her around, paying what appeared to be an excessive interest in her admittedly ample posterior. Enquiry elicited that their interest was entirely for the purpose of judging the size of the grass throne they were constructing. My mother-in-law, when this was reported to her, was vastly amused.

As we arrived, the Messenger who had been responsible for all of this, and who had obviously been on the lookout for us, was standing to attention to greet us, together with the Chief's two *kapassus* who made valiant attempts to emulate his salute. We were overwhelmed by the lavishness of our accommodation but James was not so easily satisfied and insisted on a detailed inspection accompanied by his junior before he grudgingly expressed himself satisfied.

Under James's leadership the Messengers and the *kapassus* and the labourers and, so it seemed, anyone else who happened to pass by, turned to unload our gear and erect the tent. This was no modern new-fangled tent with lightweight poles and nylon covering. This was a 'no nonsense' old-fashioned tent with heavy-weight canvas and poles the size of a man's arm and tent pegs that needed a huge mallet to drive them into the hard earth. We had just about finished this exercise when the Chief's eldest son, Mr Chulu the Health Councillor, arrived, followed by a *kapasu* carrying a washing-up bowl covered with a cloth. The purpose of the visit was firstly to deliver a present from the Chief, which the removal of the cloth revealed to be an enormous heap of very fresh meat, which the Councillor explained was a buffalo heart. It was indeed a most generous gift but I was glad that I personally did not have to deal with it.

At the same time it was suggested that it might be an appropriate moment for me to meet the Chief, who a few minutes later appeared with a small entourage of Assessors and followers. He was a charming man with the most beautiful smile. He was, like his subjects, small in stature, but wiry and although he wore European clothes he also wore a distinctive bead headdress to mark his position as the Paramount Chief of the Kunda. We used his son as an interpreter. He welcomed me to the Valley and wished me a successful tour. He asked to be kept regularly informed of the results of my tour and assured me of his cooperation. I replied, I hoped appropriately, thanking him for the gift of the buffalo heart and for his welcome and assured him that I would do my best to help him and his tribe. I then walked him back to his Palace, a brick-built house in contrast to the mud huts of his people, which was only a half-mile away from my camp.

By the time I returned, James having, of course, been in distinguished attendance, it was getting dark. Although the fire was burning, there was difficulty getting the kerosene lamps provided by the *boma* to work and it was clear from Peter's woebegone expression that he had no idea how to convert the stores we had brought with us (we had quickly decided the buffalo heart would be much more appreciated by our retainers than ourselves) into something that we could eat. My wife, excellent cook that she was, was itching to set about the task herself but it was impractical for her to try to produce a meal herself, in the dark, over an open fire, even if protocol permitted her to do so.

'Where' I demanded 'is Joey?' Joey, it appeared, had departed to the village where he had discovered a 'bruzzer'. 'Then go and get him!' I demanded. The Messengers looked doubtful.

'You mean he is drunk?' They giggled nervously. I insisted he was called. In due course Joey appeared. He was not 'drunk' but he obviously had, as the Irish would say, 'of drink taken.' I apologised for interrupting his social life and explained our difficulty, although that was all too clear even from a cursory glance. To my relief he stalked towards the chaos in the kitchen area to which, by some miracle, he quickly restored order and food was soon in the process of being produced, a miracle which, under his direction, was repeated throughout the remainder of our stay.

Joey specialised in these rescues. There was, for instance, as my mother used to tell, the occasion when she was doing a dinner party for distinguished guests, for whom it was important that the culinary boat should be well and truly pushed out. Unbeknown to her bad blood had been brewing in the kitchen between Joey the cook and the houseboy, who served at table and whom my mother had christened, within the family, 'the Bishop', due to his unusual long face and aquiline, almost Arab, features. His looks were accompanied by an air of enormous consequence which amused my father. In any event Joey had apparently been harbouring the, no doubt unworthy, suspicion that the Bishop, a younger man, had been showing more interest in Mrs Joey than was appropriate. He had, as a result of the worry of this suspicion, coupled with the strain of coping with what he realised was an important occasion, like many a cook before him, turned to the bottle for support. My mother had detected the warning signs of insobriety shortly before the guests arrived but there was nothing she could do by then except pray. The guests arrived and the Bishop served the drinks and departed to the kitchen. She began to relax. Alas for her prayers. The Bishop suddenly appeared, pursued by Joey brandishing a very large knife and showing every intention of filleting the Bishop. The guests and my father sat rooted to the spot as the Bishop sought refuge behind my mother's chair. My mother is small in stature but large in presence and in her veins ran the blood of generations of school teachers; she rose to her full height of five foot two and a quarter inches and, quelling the furious Joey with a glance, ordered him to the kitchen while my father let the Bishop out by the front door. Just as my mother was wondering whether she should go out to the kitchen to try to rescue the situation, Joey reappeared clad in his best white uniform and, ignoring what had gone before, not only cooked but served, and in style, a dinner that was all that my mother had intended.

With our commissariat organised we soon settled into life on tour. Peter would bring us tea soon after dawn so that we could take full advantage of the cool of the day. An eye was obviously kept on the progress of my breakfast because as soon as it was clear that I was back on duty, James with some relish, would draw up the Messengers, including himself as first in the line and any passing *kapassus*, for my inspection. At the same time a silent line of villagers would form just inside the *boma*. When this happened the first morning I enquired what they were waiting for and was told *mankwala* (medicine). I denied any ability to prescribe let alone provide medicines but James reassured me that the *boma* always provided a supply of medicine for its District Officers on tour. Sure enough he produced, for my inspection, a large wooden box full of jars and bottles containing evil-looking pills and potions. The task of uniting the appropriate medicines with the waiting patients was most satisfactorily solved by my wife, who although possessing no formal medical training, had enough knowledge and a strong enough stomach to set up a flourishing clinic dealing with a variety of complaints from *cifua* (cough), which could be anything from a cold to pneumonia or TB, to unstoppable diarrhoea or tropical ulcers, some of truly horrendous size. Mr Chulu in his role as Health Councillor, or one of the Messengers, translated for her. Undoubtedly her efforts were appreciated and did much to ensure our welcome in the area.

While she was administering to the sick I would set off, sometimes on foot if the villages were nearby, but more usually by bicycle to visit the villages in the Chief's area. In some Chiefs' areas it was necessary to move base halfway through the tour but the Nsefu villages were all sufficiently concentrated to allow me to cover them all from the one base camp.

Certainly to begin with we were an impressive contingent: a *kapassu* or two, James and another Messenger or two, someone to represent the Chief (an Assessor and/or Mr Chulu), the Court Clerk, who doubled as the local inspector of taxes and kept the village register, and myself, clad (in descending order) in a low-crowned bush hat, cotton khaki shirt and long cotton khaki shorts ending tastefully just above the knee, long cotton khaki socks and chukka boots. Towards the end of my tour our number would tend to diminish as weariness and boredom took their toll.

It was in fact hard work to cycle on heavy elderly sit-up-and-beg cycles that the *boma* provided over narrow tracks that consisted either of bone hard corrugations or deep sand and, as we perspired, the tsetse flies would gather in hordes on our backs. They had a vicious bite. The ordinary flies were a horror if one stopped but they soon lost interest as soon as we were on the move. The tracks meandered apparently haphazardly between the villages, through elephant grass and short wiry trees, making detours for white ant mounds, large trees and the villagers' gardens. Often the path would divide, giving rise to endless arguments

*Messengers and kapassus on parade.*

as to which was the right path to follow. The villages tended to be strung out like beads on a string and so we would start, in the comparative cool of the day, by cycling to the extremity of the string of villages and then work our way backwards. This had the advantage of ensuring that the villagers were ready for us on our return.

On my own at last and with the prospect of being in the area for the foreseeable future, I relished the opportunity of the village meetings to try to get past the initial shyness and defensiveness of the villagers and to try to engage them in a real conversation and learn about their lives and difficulties. Sometimes I would get more than I had bargained for and the Court Clerk or Messenger who was interpreting would hesitate to pass on some impassioned outburst and would need reassurance before translating a complaint about the lack of school or dispensary or (more usually in Nsefu's area) the lack of elephant or baboon control which resulted in their gardens being destroyed and 'a fat lot of notice the Chief or the *boma* took of it' they would end. I would indeed report their request for assistance to the Game Department on my return to the *boma* but it was not always easy to decide whether the villagers wanted an elephant shot to protect their gardens or for the benefit of its meat. I never minded that kind of outburst (unless it developed into mere whingeing) which was far healthier than the torpor which had stirred me to anger when touring with Bill. In exchange, of course, I would harangue them about the horror of their latrines or the lack of them, which added to the risk of illness, or the state of the paths leading to their village for the maintenance of which they were theoretically responsible. Although my youthful enthusiasm, rather like an emetic, probably did them no harm and possibly some good, I was no doubt in many instances being unfair. The check through the village register (like calling a school roll call) for the purposes of seeing who had and who had not paid their poll tax was interesting in revealing which members of the village were absent and why. Page after page of names with the response *pa ulendo* (on a journey) would, on enquiry, reveal that the villager had been away for a year or years in the Northern Rhodesian copper belt or in the mines in Southern Rhodesia and would explain the absence of any young men and why there was a slovenly village of old men and women and children. In those circumstances of bare survival it was easy to see why keeping the village clean and tidy was given a pretty low priority. The obvious answer was to keep the young men in the area but with apparently nothing other than subsistence agriculture to offer them this was easier said than done.

Like most sensible people the villagers blamed their troubles on the government. 'If only the Government would build us a dispensary we would not have so much sickness or have to waste so much time travelling to the mission hospital and we would then have more time and energy to work in our gardens' or 'if only the Government would give us a road the lorries could get in to collect our grain and take it to market which it is impossible for us to do at present on the handlebars of our bicycles.' So the arguments would run. This would be in the 'good' villages where at least they had a desire to improve their lot. In the 'bad' they would be too apathetic even to complain. If it was a scheme that was within the competence of the Native Authority I would raise the request with the Chief and/or the Kunda Native Authority. If it required central Government assistance I would raise it with the appropriate department on my return to the *boma*. In either case the answer was always the same – that 'there is not enough money to do everything and your request must take its turn.' I found, however, that it would help my argument if I could report that the villagers had already tried to do something to implement the scheme. As a result I adopted the slogan and went around preaching that 'the Government helps those who help themselves', 'Government' being, in this context, interchangeable between central or local government. I did achieve some success with this policy so that for instance, in relation to a new dispensary, an offer by the villagers to clear the site and make the mud bricks would elicit an offer to provide the cement and window and door frames and roof from the Kunda Native Authority (under pressure from me) and the reluctant agreement from the Health Department to provide a Health Assistant and a supply of basic drugs.

By early afternoon the sun would be high and it would be a hard slog even for a fit 23-year-old to cycle in the heat. Hopefully, however, the day's work had been well planned so that the final visit could be completed in time for us to return to our temporary *boma* for a cup of tea and a siesta for what remained of the afternoon, before emerging for a thoroughly unsatisfactory splash in the canvas bath. This does a gross injustice to the water and wood carriers who were heroic in their efforts to heat enough water in old petrol cans to give us a bath in the evening. However, even four inches of murky water in a piece of four-foot by four-foot green canvas sitting on the bare earth with the corners kept erect by wooden pegs was, in the circumstances, better than nothing and a treat to be looked forward to in the cool of the evening. We would wallow contentedly ignoring the attempts of the local children to peep through the grass walls and disprove the ridiculous rumour that we were white all over.

After that there was time to sit in the very brief twilight to watch the sun set in a blaze of colour and enjoy a beer as a 'sundowner'. This was the time that James would cough discreetly from the shadows and wait to be invited in for a beer and a post-mortem on the day and to plan the campaign for the morrow. To begin with we had to call in one of the other younger Messengers to interpret for us but both of us found this frustrating and I soon learned enough Chinyanja so that on subsequent tours I could communicate with him in that language. James was very patient with my efforts and seemed happy to repeat as many times as I needed what I had not understood. On occasions his rudimentary English came to our assistance although very soon I spoke better Chinyanja than he did English.

One of our first subjects of conversation on this first tour was the matter of *nyama* (meat) for the labourers which James assured me was becoming urgent. Unsurprisingly the wood *nyama* is also the word for 'wild animal'. It was obviously pure oversight that made him omit to mention that the lion's share of any meat that might be in the offing would go to the Messengers and of that share the first part would, by right of his seniority, go to James. I protested that I had no rifle, that I was no shot, that I had no experience of shooting in the wild and finally that I had no idea where in the area to start looking for edible game. James dealt indulgently with these trifling objections The ancient .303 rifle that we had brought with us from the *boma* might not be a hunting rifle but it had seen service in the war (which we had won) and so it must be all right. As for my lack of experience and expertise, all that I needed was a bit of practice and the assistance of a good local hunter who, by pure coincidence, had only recently returned from a successful hunting expedition and was waiting outside. He would be delighted to show me where I could find any number of edible animals who would be only too pleased to present themselves to me for an easy shot and with the minimum of inconvenience to myself.

Thus it was that some time before dawn the next day I found myself nervously following the slight figure of the renowned hunter to whom I had been introduced by James the previous evening. Any doubts as to his competence quickly disappeared as he led me at a brisk walk across the plain dotted with small trees which showed up against the rapidly lightening sky. From the scrunch under our feet the grass had apparently been burned and indeed as full light came I saw that, except for a few surviving patches of tall elephant grass, the plain across which we were travelling was as flat as a billiard board and apart from the scrubby little trees just about as open. Although I was soon sweating heavily and panting at the pace my guide set, he (clad in the tattered remains of a singlet and shorts and barefooted) appeared entirely at his ease gliding effortlessly where I stumbled. Every now and then he would remove a scrap of cloth from the pocket of his tattered shorts and shake it slightly so as to release a little of the fine sand he had apparently secreted in it, thereby showing him the direction of the wind. After an hour or so of this, and just when I was beginning to congratulate myself that there was no game to be had so that my skill as a hunter would go untested, the hunter pointed at what seemed to be hoof prints (we had no means of communicating except by signs) apparently leading towards a clump of tall mopane trees and long grass. 'Njati, Bwana!' he whispered excitedly, which I recognised as meaning buffalo. He did not wait for me to protest that I had no intention of taking on a buffalo, which hardly qualified in my book as 'shooting for the pot' but set off apace towards the trees, giving me no alternative but to follow him. As we got closer to the trees, I noticed large mounds of dung, some of it ominously recently laid. The hunter now began to tiptoe forward towards an apparently impenetrable wall of grass and reeds, obviously a watercourse, which explained the tall trees. We had been approaching this down an avenue between the trees which grew close together in this area, he on one side and me on the other. He gestured to me across the avenue to get ready and I obediently put a bullet in the breech of my rifle which I held in the high port position. He moved cautiously forward a few more yards and then took cover behind a patch of grass looking across towards me to make sure I was following his example. I kneeled with the rifle held uncertainly in front of me. There was a strong smell of rank animal and the sounds of a large digestive system apparently complaining to itself. The hunter across the way unnecessarily pointed at the reeds and put a finger to his lips to indicate I should be silent. I was very conscious of my breath rasping in my throat. I tried to quieten it. There was nothing I could do about the trip hammer in my chest. Suddenly there was a crash to my left, indicating that a large animal had broken cover. I readied myself, if waving the rifle in the approximate direction of the commotion qualifies as such. The hunter could see 'it' before I could. To my relief he gestured vigorously not to shoot and when a large bull rhino a few seconds later trotted purposefully past me I entirely understood his caution. I still ponder what I would have done if it had been a buffalo that had appeared. I like to imagine I would have had the nerve to put a bullet neatly between its eyes but I have to confess that my instinct for self-preservation would probably have got the better of me.

In any event we resumed our increasingly hot trek across the plain in search of something to shoot. It was I who first spotted what appeared to be a small black dust cloud moving swiftly in our general direction through the trees and over the black remains of the recent grass burning. The hunter shaded his eyes against the glare and then immediately called urgently 'Tawani, Bwana, Tawani!' I had no idea what he said but the urgency was obvious and he reinforced what was clearly a warning by shinning swiftly up the nearest tree. I hesitated a second or two to try to see the danger and to assess whether it was sufficiently dire to merit losing my dignity to the extent of climbing a tree. The hesitation was nearly my undoing. There was a hollow drumming noise on the rock hard earth and I saw only few yards away a rhino, presumably the same we had previously disturbed, heading at a hand-gallop precisely in my direction. He had clearly scented me. I very briefly pondered the wisdom of keeping hold of my rifle, but there was no time for such courtesies as I sprang for the nearest tree, up which I shinned so fast that in no time my head protruded from the top. From this point of vantage I was relieved to see the rhino pounding off into the middle distance, head up trying to regain the scent which he had lost when I had unsportingly climbed the tree.

After this, by cumbersome but heartfelt pantomime, I persuaded my guide that we should concentrate on finding some smaller and less challenging quarry than a buffalo or, for that matter, a rhino. In due course we did indeed find some type of antelope which obligingly stood still long enough for me to slay him and thus slake the hunger of my followers for fresh meat and salvage some shreds of my reputation as a hunter.

We returned eventually to the *boma*, in my case hot and exhausted, to find my wife absorbed in finishing her clinic.

'I got charged by a rhino,' I reported.

'Did it hit you?'

'No.'

'Oh, that's all right then.'

Our tour ended a few days later. We waited with mixed feelings for the lorry to come and collect our *katundu* (luggage) and return us and it to Fort Jimmy, where I had to spend the next few weeks writing up my Tour Report which, with umpteen copies, had to be submitted to the District Commissioner for onward transmission to the Provincial Commissioner and Lusaka.

At Fort Jimmy we were at last allocated a house and we moved with relief into our first home. This was a pleasant bungalow high up on one of the hills that surrounded the town. It had two bedrooms, albeit one scarcely more than a boxroom. It had an established garden and a small servants' house at the bottom of the back garden, which provided palatial accommodation for the bachelor Peter. It had been completely re-decorated and came with a sparse but adequate complement of Government-manufactured furniture (wooden Morris-style armchairs and sofa with rawhide strings instead of springs). One bought one's own cushions and covers which were run up by the Indian tailors. The disadvantages of the bungalow were that it was as far away from the shops as it was possible to be which, without a car, we found was a substantial problem. In addition it occupied a corner plot, which meant, with earth roads, that it was always dusty. It also meant that it tempted the local Africans to cut the corner across our front garden. Cool reflection told me that it was their country and their culture did not recognise privately-owned gardens and that it was second nature to expend the minimum of energy and so to cut corners. Such thoughts I confess were far from my mind when for the umpteenth time a line of women (used to narrow tracks through the bush they always walked in a line) with bundles on their heads and children slung on their backs perambulated gently past the windows of our sitting room while we had friends in for a sundowner (the traditional drinks party at sunset). It was largely to deter these invasions, as well as to give my wife some comfort while I was away so often on tour, that we found a new and important recruit to our establishment in the person of a dachshund whom I christened Dixon Oliver Goddard or District OfficerG for short in moments of stress or strife. This was no dainty neurotic little morsel to sit on one's knee but a large, distinctly butch chap afraid of nothing and nobody, to whom we rapidly became devoted. He also, as soon as he became old enough to bark, solved our trespasser problem. He adored to ambush a line of women and to see them scatter squawking like chickens. A few passages like this and the word soon appeared to have gone round to give our garden a wide berth.

As I was soon so much away on tour in the valley, the lack of transport was more of a problem for my wife who had by now started work at the Education Department, which was a good half-hour's walk away. In practice I believe she usually got a lift from someone in her office but nonetheless it was an irritation having to worry how to get to work or to the shops where she very soon got on terms with Mr Deya and his brethren at the other Indian stores. I happened to be present on one of their first passages of arms. The traders did not encourage bargaining

*Dixon Oliver Goddard (DOG) with friend.*

except with the Africans and on their own terms but if pushed would reluctantly be prepared to give a little discount. My wife beat Mr Deya down to giving not a little but a substantial discount on some large item and then as a final twist demanded and extracted from a thoroughly demoralised Mr Deya an additional two and a half per cent 'for cash'.

'Thank you,' she smiled sweetly. 'Please put it on my account' and sailed out.

Although her work at the Education Department prevented her, except occasionally, coming on tour with me (which anyway she would have found uncomfortable and boring after the novelty of the first tour) she did enjoy coming with me to the Nsefu Game Reserve.

Back in Fort Jimmy we got to know our neighbours. On one side was an elderly Scots couple with strong Glaswegian accents, he an engineer in the PWD and an obsessive gardener, she a tiny, energetic, homely body who loved to mother us and was forever giving us little gifts of food. Communication was on occasions difficult. I still treasure the look of blank incomprehension on my wife's face when our neighbour brought over the fruit cake she had just cooked for us, announcing proudly in her thick Glaswegian accent, 'Ah made sure it wuz well-fired so ah ken that it's no' soggy i' the muddle.'

On the other side was a middle-aged couple who were starting a new life in Northern Rhodesia (he as a locally-recruited clerk in the Ministry of Agriculture) having lost everything tobacco farming in Southern Rhodesia. Their resilience was incredible and we became very fond of them and exchanged hospitality. We also kept in touch with Jim whose wife had by now joined him, and we exchanged visits, they to the Valley and we to Chadiza. To them Fort Jimmy, despite its deficiencies, was 'the City' and they visited us more than we visited them, as they were always anxious to see the bright lights and stock up on the stores that were unobtainable in their outstation. One of their first visits coincided with an invitation to a sundowners party at the District Commissioner's house in which they were included. They arrived in a flat-bed lorry to collect stores for their District Commissioner. It was not an ideal vehicle in which to go to a smart party but it was infinitely better than walking and so, at the appointed hour, the girls in their party frocks were manoeuvred into the front of the lorry to sit on Jim's lap, he having suggested I drive as I knew the way to the District Commissioner's house. I was rather proud of the way I handled a lorry for the first time until we drove down the drive into the District Commissioner's house when I attempted to brake, only to realise that a lorry and particularly that lorry did not stop as quickly as a Land-Rover. The house was set above the garden on top of a grassy man-made mound where the District Commissioner and his charming wife and a little crowd of guests watched with amazement and then alarm as, unable to stop the lorry in the parking area without hitting the already parked cars, I turned the lorry towards the mound, hoping that the slope would stop the lorry's apparently irresistible progress. It did but not before the crowd of guests had thought discretion the better part of valour and retreated rapidly towards the veranda. We dismounted with such dignity as we could muster to greet the District Commissioner who was sadly contemplating the unsightly ruts the lorry had made to his carefully tended lawn.

Jim and his wife were also invited with us to a dinner party for sixteen that the Provincial Commissioner hosted soon after our arrival. We all sat comfortably around the enormous, heavy, locally-made wooden table in the huge dining room of his official residence which, with its vast rooms with high ceilings and deep verandas and gardens the size of a park, had obviously been built at the time that Fort Jimmy was founded.

'Well,' the Provincial Commissioner barked at the end of dinner, 'was that all right or shall I beat the cook?' We laughed nervously (one could never tell whether or not the Provincial Commissioner was joking) but his long-time cook Sixpence did not look too worried.

The Provincial Commissioner's residence was the scene some months later for an evening garden party given by the Provincial Commissioner for the Governor and his Lady who were on an official visit to Fort Jimmy and, of course, were staying with the Provincial Commissioner. The garden party was a large affair and not only were the European heads of department and their assistants and wives invited but also the local Paramount Chiefs and the senior officer of their Native Authority and, I think, an Assessor or two. The Kunda were duly invited and as their District Officer I was invited along to look after them. I suggested that they foregather at our bungalow for a drink before the party, for the dual purpose of showing hospitality and also ensuring that we all arrived at the party at the same time. They duly arrived at the appointed hour, beautifully turned out with the Chief resplendent in his distinctive bead headgear. Drinks were served and it quickly became apparent that the Chief, nervous at the idea of attending such a distinguished gathering, had as an antidote to this 'of drink taken'. Gentleman that he was, however, he had in no way lost his manners and as usual he behaved with courtesy and charm. He did, however, speak in a slightly incoherent fashion and it was obvious he had some difficulty in focusing.

For obvious reasons I did not offer a second drink and we set off, in the Land-Rover organised for the occasion, to the party. The extensive grounds of the Provincial Commissioner's residence were bright with lights; a clever touch had been to fill brown paper bags with sand into which candles had been stuck. The paper bags not only protected the candles from any breeze but the light of the candles through the brown paper created a most attractive effect. There was a large crowd of the Province's finest, all in their party best, with an army of servants in white uniforms to hand around trays of drinks and canapés. Being somewhat self-conscious of acting as custodian to an inebriated Chief, we passed swiftly down the reception line and took our bearings. There were a number of people we already knew, including the farmer I had met in less formal circumstances, who was kind enough to smile faintly in recognition in my direction. Otherwise it was mainly departmental heads whom, as very new and insignificant arrivals, we mainly knew only by sight. My colleagues from the *boma* whom I knew best, namely District Officer Ngoni and District Officer Chewa were, like myself, shepherding groups of Chiefs and Councillors and, like ourselves, were finding that it is not easy to mingle mob-handed. I tried to suggest to the Chief that it might be better if we split up, but he went into such a panic at the suggestion – like a drowning man seizing my arm in a vice-like grip – that I abandoned the attempt and we spent the remainder of the evening making desultory conversation with the Administrative Councillor. Although he spoke excellent English and was very happy to translate for the Chief and myself, the Chief, provided he remained attached to my arm, seemed happy just to look about him and smile indulgently at anyone who looked in his direction. By the time we had to join the line that was bidding farewell to the Governor and his wife, the Chief was thoroughly enjoying himself, but showing no intention at all of releasing my arm. Thus it was that when, at last, we approached the Governor, I had my wife on one arm and the beaming Chief on the other, with the remainder of the Kunda nervously bringing up the rear. Giving a sort of bow to the Governor's party, I made to move thankfully out into the darkness but the Chief would have none of this modern informality. Leaving hold of my arm, and instead seizing my hand, he fell upon his knees and began going through what I presumed was the full, old-fashioned obeisance made by a tribesman to his Chief in thanks that the Chief has just decided against impaling him on a pointed stake (or whatever Kunda chiefs used to do to entertain their visitors). It involved a great deal of what I think is called ululating. I could only stand, sweating with embarrassment, and no doubt grinning like a fool. I need not have worried, however; the performance was greeted with obvious delight by the Governor and his wife and indeed by the considerable crowd that formed around us. The Chief had no sooner hauled himself to his feet with my assistance at the end than, realising how well he had been received, he immediately repeated the whole thing all over again and showed every intention of doing a second encore had I not physically dragged him away. Shortly afterwards I received congratulations from my mother at having given the Governor's party such a moving welcome, she having received what was obviously a highly-coloured account from the Governor's wife, with whom she was on coffee-morning terms, on the latter's return to Lusaka.

In fact my parents, who returned to Lusaka from leave a few months after our arrival in Fort Jimmy, visited us soon after their return to satisfy themselves, no doubt, that all was indeed well with us. They travelled up in their own car, which was no small undertaking as there were 300 terrible corrugated miles over the Great East Road between Lusaka and Fort Jimmy. Their visit ironically caused the departure of Peter. He was beginning to learn his trade (although it was hard going) but we began to have worries about his activities off duty. He was a clever young man with a cheeky, engaging character who was obviously having a ball away from home for the first time. There were several occasions when he came on duty obviously the worse for wear and, as the police would say, 'he was warned as to his conduct.' In celebration of their visit we had bravely invited the Provincial Commissioner to dine, he and my parents being old friends. In those days I did not drink whisky but we always kept a bottle in the house for the visit of senior officers who, like the Provincial Commissioner, drank nothing else (very weak and with soda). I was not, therefore, aware, until just before the Provincial Commissioner's arrival and after the Indian stores had closed, that there was a bare inch left in the whisky bottle that I remembered being virtually full. Peter, under vigorous cross-examination, admitted his guilt but that did not solve the problem of what to give the Provincial Commissioner when he arrived in half an hour's time looking forward to a Scotch. Happily my father, when the problem was reported to him, made light of the matter and, after a brief absence, reappeared with a bottle of Scotch, coincidentally of precisely the brand that our enquiries had elicited was the Provincial Commissioner's favourite. I was too bothered at the time and during the very pleasant evening that ensued, to enquire by what magic my father had conjured up the bottle of precisely the right Scotch. It was not until several days later, when I tried unsuccessfully to settle up with my father, that I learned he had solved the problem very easily by driving round to the Provincial Commissioner's house and borrowing a bottle from Sixpence, which of course he subsequently replaced. It was in any event the end of Peter, who was dismissed and packed off back to the Northern Province. We did not want the responsibility of having him roistering around the township where the local Chewa and Ngoni lads would sooner or later have felt it necessary to take down a peg a Bemba lad who was so popular with the girls.

He was replaced, albeit at considerable additional expense, by a proper experienced cook called Sampson. Sampson was, I suppose, in his late fifties or early sixties and had recently taken unto himself a very much younger wife who, soon after Sampson started with us, presented him with an adorable baby son. Sampson was rightly proud of and devoted to both wife and son. By this time I was away from the *boma* on tour in the Valley so often that there was no avoiding the need for me to have my own touring cook who would double up as houseboy when I was briefly at home. And so Phiri joined us and stayed with us, as indeed did Sampson, until we left the Eastern Province. This additional expense was the justification for the touring allowances that I could claim when I was away from the *boma*.

Perhaps this is an appropriate moment to say something about the servants that we, the expatriate officers, employed. In these liberated times I can imagine the pursed lips and muttering about exploitation at the idea that a young couple, barely out of their teens, should employ not one but two or three servants to do work that in England we would have done ourselves. The first point, of course, is that the heat made it impractical for the English housewife, or for that matter husband, to do heavy physical work. Secondly, the houses in which we lived did not have the labour-saving devices that we take for granted in England so that, for instance, the stove on which we cooked our food was wood-fired as was the hot water system. Wood was freely available and the *boma* lorry used to deliver a load of logs on request. The huge logs which they delivered had then to be chopped up into sizes that would fit into the kitchen stove and into the void under the 44-gallon oil drum, suspended on two brick pillars outside the bathroom and connected to it with a metal tube, in which our bath water was heated. There was electricity in Fort Jimmy, which ran the lights, but it was pretty unreliable because we always remained loyal to our paraffin-driven refrigerator. The standard remedy for curing any problems with the refrigerator was to wrap it in a blanket and roll it around on the floor. The irons for pressing our clothes were either huge great machines that were filled with charcoal from the kitchen stove or else a team of heavy flatirons that were heated on the top of the stove and used in turn so that as one was being used the other was heating up.

To do this heavy work the Europeans, be they civil servants or settlers, would employ servants (in my time never women, except to act as nannies). These personal servants were always called 'boys', as in the sentence 'Will you take your boys with you when you move to the Southern Province?' It is, I agree, a demeaning term to apply to men who were very often of middle age. Some had been with a family, as had Joey for instance with mine, for twenty years or more and carried considerable responsibility. They were furthermore treated with affection and respect, not only by the family for whom they worked but by the friends of the family to whom, over the years, they had become very well-known. However, the term had become so accepted, even by the servants themselves, that it was impossible to change.

What we did not do was to address them, or indeed any African, as 'boy'. I say it was never done but in truth it was done, mainly by Europeans of South African origin and, I have to say, by the Indians. It sounded terrible and was no doubt deeply and justifiably resented. I, and I guess my colleagues in the Eastern Province, would address strangers as *Bambo*, and *Azimai* if female. Both words are in the plural, which was a way of showing respect, and roughly translate as 'mister' and 'mother'.

How many did you employ, I hear you ask, and how much did you pay them? The answer to the first of these questions is that it depended on the size of one's establishment and the depth of one's pocket. My father, as head of department, expected to do a fair amount of entertaining, both of friends and colleagues in the provincial capital and of those coming up from Lusaka on government business. My parents, therefore, would need a cook, and a kitchen boy to help him. They would also need a houseboy, both to do the cleaning around the house (there was always a lot of dust and the floors were all cement, painted and kept polished red) and to serve at table. Finally there was a garden boy, not only to do the garden, which included watering night and morning, but also to cut the firewood for the kitchen and the bathwater.

A small establishment such as ours would normally have employed only a cook, who would also do the housework (with considerable assistance from my wife) and a garden boy-cum-kitchen boy. Because I was away so much and needed someone to look after me on tour, we had in effect two cooks, one senior and one junior. They did not clash, partly because they were both nice sensible men and partly because they only rarely worked under one roof. Phiri, back in the house for a few days, would happily take a turn doing the dusting and polishing and serving at table, as well as doing my touring washing and getting the touring kitchen boxes ready for going out again. In addition there was a succession of garden-cum-kitchen boys of whom I confess I have not the slightest memory.

How much did we pay? I cannot remember the details but I do recall that the total bill I calculated once was about a quarter of my monthly salary, which was rather less than £90. In addition to their wages, we also provided uniform, khaki drill short-sleeved bush jacket and shorts or long trousers (at their choice) with a little pillbox-type hat for every day and the equivalent in white for the evenings. Phiri chose shorts for his khaki outfit and the older Sampson long trousers for both. They were also provided with accommodation, in our case in the form of a one-roomed hut in the back garden with washroom and toilet. They were pretty rudimentary in our terms but were considerably better than the thatched mud and wattle huts that they would have had in their villages. They were also provided with 'rations', consisting each week of meat, sugar, salt, I think cooking oil, and certainly two types of soap, one for washing their uniforms and the other for bathing. They provided their own *nshima* (flour), in our area made from maize. I seem to remember bringing in sacks of flour for the servants but perhaps my Land-Rover simply provided the transport for what they had found and bought themselves. Perhaps it was during a period of shortage when we had a better chance of finding an honest source of supply than they could, being cut off from their home villages.

For this they worked a long day from 6.30 a.m. (I think) until after lunch when they would disappear until early evening; they would then come in to serve drinks and dinner – except, that is, for the garden boy, who would come in an hour or so earlier to get the fire going for the baths, and light up the stove ready for the cook to start preparing dinner. The duties of the garden boy were fairly elastic, depending on the views of the cook and the ambition of the garden boy. A keen garden boy would be anxious to get into the house or at least into the kitchen where, in exchange for washing up, he would learn something of the duties of the cook and houseboy. I certainly have visions of our garden boys happily helping out in the kitchen under Sampson's directions on dinner party evenings.

*Cook Sampson and son.*

In any event this was our establishment and we gave little thought to the rights and wrongs of the situation. I guess if we had been asked to explain the justification for having servants, we would simply have replied that 'as a representative of government we were expected to maintain a certain standard and servants were necessary to do that.' And anyway it provided a considerable number of the local population with moderately honest employment. What is certain is that we became very fond of and concerned for our little team and I believe they became genuinely fond of us. Indeed the only occasion I can ever remember that we fell out was when we invited the wife of one of the African Cadets who had been on the course with me to lunch. He was an Ngoni, I recall, and had been posted (perhaps as a matter of policy) to another province. His wife was a lovely, educated girl whom we had met in England and we were delighted to invite her for a meal when we heard she was going to visit Fort Jimmy to see her family. However, when we told Sampson and Phiri whom we had invited to lunch, they were not amused and asked for an assurance that they would not have to serve a black woman. In vain did we explain that her husband was exactly of my rank and furthermore a time would come, and pretty soon at that, when the majority of District Officers would be African and it would be natural for their wives to be given the same respect as they gave to the wives of my European colleagues who visited the house. In the end they capitulated when we insisted that our African friend would have lunch with us and if they did not want to serve her then we would serve her ourselves. They did so and gradually thawed under our guest's charm, she probably understanding far better than we did why, to begin with, Phiri particularly 'had his ears back'.

# CHAPTER 4

# In the Valley

THE STAR IN THE Kunda Native Authority crown was the Nsefu Game Reserve. It was unique in that it had been dedicated, free of charge, to the Government by one of the predecessors of Chief Nsefu, but on terms that it was to remain under the control, and for the benefit, of the Kunda Native Authority. Although the Native Authority employed the civilian staff to run the 'hotel' side of the camp, and although I encouraged the Councillors to visit the camp from time to time (usually in my company and in my transport) it was left to me, as District Officer Kunda, to supervise the camp and provide the stores of tins and other essentials, which the staff sold to and cooked for visitors who had either not understood the situation, or had otherwise not had the forethought to bring their own. The Game Guards and their supervision were provided by the Game Department based in Fort Jimmy.

There were other camps up and down the Luangwa, both in Fort Jimmy district and upstream in Lundazi district. Some of these, such as the Norman Carr Camp at M'fuwe, were privately run. Others, such as Chilongozi in Chief Malama's area, were Government run, with a resident European Game Warden. Nsefu was the only Native Authority run camp and the Kunda were rightly proud of it and grateful to me for supervising it for them. Unfortunately the Nsefu Game Camp could not be accessed easily from the rest of the Kunda valley. There was a 'Land-Rover track' but it ran across a flood plain, which made it so excruciatingly uncomfortable, even for one who was soon inured to uncomfortable roads, that I only used it in dire necessity. Being at the end of the road I could not, therefore, visit it on the way to do something else and I accordingly took to visiting it at weekends, which had the advantage that I could take my wife with me. It also had the advantage that as I got paid a subsistence allowance for every night that I spent away from Fort Jimmy on Government business I could perfectly legitimately claim for my nights at weekends spent in the Reserve. The second season I was there I organised to have built a small grass *boma* on a bluff just above the camp. Although it meant we had to use campbeds instead of the proper beds in the guest rooms, it made us independent of the camp and its staff and was anyway much more pleasant.

The Nsefu Game Camp was a magical place. It was built on a high bank on the inside of a bend in the Luangwa River, which at that point was very wide, giving a panoramic view over the river and the wild life that came down to drink in the early morning and evening. Its real magic, for me and for most of the guests who visited, was that the game viewing was on foot. That, and the fact that there was no resident European supervision, made it easy to imagine that one was on one's own in Africa, just as it must have been when the English adventurers first found their way to the area. We soon became entirely comfortable at being the only white faces for a hundred miles but I often marvelled at the courage of the visitors, admittedly mainly from Northern and Southern Rhodesia, but with a substantial minority from Europe, who in hired motorcars would venture over awful roads on a tour through the Game Camps. At Nsefu they could well be the only visitors, and be entirely on their own with the two or three camp staff and similar number of Game Guards. There was, of course, no electricity and visitors were reliant on paraffin lamps and torches. There were no 'en suite' facilities and, as wandering hippos were regular visitors, a final visit to the 'facilities' before retiring was strongly recommended.

Despite these shortcomings, or perhaps because of them, the camp was always popular and the Visitors' Book, which I read avidly on my visits, was full of praise from people who appreciated its lack of amenities and liked the feeling of seeing nature in the raw. There were inevitably the occasional whinges as well as some genuine complaints. One, I remember particularly, was from an elderly lady who suggested that it might be a good idea either to keep the hippo further away from the camp or, if this was not possible, to move the camp further back from the river, as the noise that the hippos made at night had disturbed her rest. The expeditions in the mornings or evenings with the Game Guards (in their grey green uniforms and bush hats) for us made up for any discomfort. On our weekend visits we would be on our own, or occasionally with friends, and the Guards would take us out on foot for a couple of hours. The terrain was mainly a continuation of the open country, with sparse trees, where I had met my rhino. Near the river, however, were pools of water left over, presumably, from the annual floods, where there was bright green grass and proper tall trees looking like some divine English parkland through which herds of impala would flicker and where families of elephant could be seen at very close quarters. I never saw any lion at Nsefu but I did see cheetah and there was a very full complement of the usual herbivores such as buffalo, rhino, zebra, eland and the rest. There were no giraffe, which could only be found at Chilongozi.

On occasions I would visit the Camp mid-week during 'office hours' as it were, in which event James would insist on coming with us on these walks, discarding for this purpose his hat and bush jacket (but alas not his army boots) and appearing in his grey undershirt and blue shorts. He seemed to enjoy these expeditions enormously but his wolfish grin and the way he would imitate aiming a rifle whenever we approached an edible species made me rather suspicious of his sentiments. There must have been some poaching around the fringes of the Reserve but I do not remember it being the problem that it clearly was in some African countries. Perhaps it has changed now. I hope not. I believe that the fact that it was their own Kunda Reserve may well have persuaded the Akunda to keep their distance.

The main problem in the reserve was the elephants that did enormous damage to the trees and also broke out (there was, of course, nothing to stop them) and caused horrendous damage to the gardens of the nearby villages. There were no villages 'near' the reserve but, of course, elephants can travel long distances if they have a mind to do so. They had the knack of knowing exactly the moment when the maize was just ready to harvest and would move in. The villagers, whose subsistence agriculture made their very existence dependent on their harvest, would do their utmost to deter the elephants. There would be rickety little watchtowers built around the gardens for the young men and boys of the village to live in during the harvest period to give warning of the approach of the elephants. Fires would be lit and drums banged when the elephants were known to be in the area. Sometimes this was not enough and the word would go out for the Game Department to send out a marksman to chase away the marauders or on occasions to shoot the offender. Then of course the villagers would obtain some compensation for their damaged gardens from the meat they could scavenge from the enormous corpse. I attended one such occasion, having been put on notice from the groups of villagers I saw hurrying along with empty bowls and containers on their heads, and with hatchets and pangas in their hands. Enquiry elicited that a large elephant had been killed and they were on their way to get their share of the meat. And sure enough a few miles further on we found the carcase of a large elephant. The tusks had been removed by the Game Guard and taken to the *boma*, leaving the huge carcase to be hacked up and carted away by the villagers who, from miles away, were hurrying to claim their share of the windfall. It was not a sight for anyone with a delicate stomach. The villagers, stripped to their bare essentials, had already hacked off the thick outer skin on one side of the beast and were crawling all over the animal, hacking off huge chunks of flesh which they were passing down to their womenfolk to put in the bowls and containers to take back to their village. A large hole had been excavated in the chest cavity and some enterprising, and not too squeamish, character had crawled inside to get at the internal organs which no doubt had a high culinary value. I was not tempted to linger very long but it was, needless to say, long enough for James to acquire a substantial lump of meat, which at my insistence, he stowed away in the back of the Land-Rover. For the next few weeks every village within ten miles of the kill had racks of very smelly elephant meat drying in the sun.

My own personal complaint about the elephants was their unfortunate habit of ambushing me on the road. We would be making our way back to the *boma* at the end of a hot exhausting day, making our best speed over the truly awful road over the flood plain, which formed the outer part of the Reserve, when suddenly out from behind a tree a large grey shape would appear, huge head rotating ominously in the direction of the Land-Rover. Whoever was driving, sometimes myself, sometimes a Messenger driver, would brake viciously and a cloud of dust would billow over the Land-Rover. It was no doubt this dust that saved us because it prevented the elephant seeing what it was that had appeared to irritate him. In this respite the Land-Rover would be put in reverse and a hasty retreat beaten to a safe distance back down the track to wait for the beast to move away. Sometimes he or she would move only a few yards off the track. Then one would move carefully forward, with the people in the back (there were always people in the back) keeping an eye out from their point of vantage for any sign of the beast making towards us. Then at the last minute one would accelerate hard and roar past, heart beating. We had some very close shaves of this kind. I had a very healthy respect for the damage that elephants could do, having seen the wreck of a Land-Rover belonging to a political leader who had been touring in the Valley and had reversed too slowly away from an elephant, who was obviously not of his political persuasion. The devastation caused to the vehicle was truly awesome and although I was not sorry to see the 'opposition' thus discomforted, I could not but sympathise with him at the unpleasantness of the experience.

My most unnerving experience of elephant occurred when I was on foot. I had been touring in Malama's area just outside the Chilongozi reserve. Unusually, my wife was with me and we had visited the young Game Warden who was resident there for a sundowner. It was needless to say dark when I left. We had James with us, of course, and a couple of local villagers, to whom we were giving a lift, and a Messenger driver. Just outside the Reserve we ran off the road. No one was hurt but we were all rather shaken. The wheels were well and truly jammed and try as we would we could not extract the vehicle. There was nothing for it but to walk down the road in the dark to the nearest village and hopefully recruit enough muscle to lift the Land-Rover out. We set off, leaving the Messenger driver to protect the vehicle. It was pitch dark without a moon but our eyes soon became sufficiently adjusted for us to see the light-coloured surface of the road and we made good progress. I then became aware of animal noises in the bush not far ahead. A whisper from one of the villagers, translated by James, confirmed my fears that it was an elephant. I had brought the *boma* rifle with me from its usual position behind the front seats in the Land-Rover. Its presence may have been good for the morale of the rest of the party but I was well aware that, in the absence of being able to see even the outline of the beast, it was of absolutely no use in our predicament. There was nothing for it but to press on. We moved cautiously on, the villagers silently in their bare feet, myself softly in my rubber-soled chukka boots and James extremely noisily in his army-issue boots. It appeared to me there was only one animal, a few yards to our right, and it was, from the noise of ripping vegetation, apparently feeding. We got closer and I contemplated returning to the Land-Rover until the moon came up but pride drove me on. I unslung the rifle and did my usual act of waving it in the general direction of the elephant. We tiptoed on. Now we could hear his stomach rumbling as he digested the leaves, or whatever it was that he was eating, and we could even smell him. Every now and then the noise of eating would stop and we would freeze until it started again. Eventually we were past and the noise and scent disappeared safely behind us. In due course we reached the village and, as a bonus, found a vehicle in the village whose driver willingly drove us and an enthusiastic crowd of villagers back to our Land-Rover which was lifted bodily out of the bush. With a bit of a brush down it and the relieved driver took us safely back to camp and a very welcome beer.

In the Valley I charged around introducing myself to all and sundry and investigating everything, whether it was my business or not. Looking back, I must have been rather like an over-enthusiastic puppy, wagging his tail frantically, convinced that everyone was a friend and pleased to see him and constantly pushing his nose into places it would have been much safer not to have pushed it. So in addition to visiting Nsefu Game Camp, I visited the other camps. At Chilongozi I found the resident Game Warden whom I have just mentioned. He was not much older than myself and lived on his own most of the year, apart from the visitors, of course. With him I quickly established a friendship and made sure I had a crate of Castle beer (the Southern Rhodesia lager that was the staple long drink of the country) whenever I was in his area so that I would not visit him empty-handed. I also visited the Norman Carr Camp where I received a distinctly frosty reception from the Great Man on the lines of 'Thank you for paying your respects but if you don't mind please go and play elsewhere as we are busy.'

Similarly I went to see the missionaries, starting with the White Fathers, who had a pleasant red-brick mission just outside Jumbe from which the three resident Fathers would travel the Valley. They were welcoming and hospitable and fun. The senior was a charming man, Father DeVere, a Dutchman, who seemed to spend most of his time in and around Jumbe. He was particularly fond of the ford at Jumbe which was a few hundred yards on the Luangwa side of the Indian stores. The ford, a concrete roadway placed across the bed of a small river, a tributary of the Luangwa, was part of the main road down to the main part of the Kunda area and the Luangwa and the Game Camps. During the dry period it was unremarkable, with the merest trickle of water finding its way through the dry white sand of the river-bed. During the rains it became a river a foot or so deep which could easily be forded on foot or by vehicle. After a heavy downpour, however, it could, in a very short time, become a raging torrent which could, and during my time did, wash away a flat-bed lorry loaded with sacks of maize which unwisely relied upon its weight to protect it from the force of the water. On several occasions I had distinctly clammy palms as the water reached the tailboard of my Land-Rover and I could feel the force of the water pushing the Land-Rover towards the edge of the concrete which was marked by poles of an ominous height. It was here on the bank, particularly during the rainy season, that Father De Vere in his distinctive white cassock would take station, greeting and chatting with the villagers as they crossed the ford.

He had two colleagues, one a German and the other a Frenchman, a perfect scenario, as I would point out, for a dirty joke or limerick. Indeed the White Fathers were known as, and they encouraged the world to call them, the Crazy Gang. Whenever I visited they would insist on opening a crate of beer, claiming that they were delighted to have a guest as an excuse to do so. They would visit us when they were in Fort Jimmy because, as they said, the food was so much better than in the mission just outside the town where they were meant to go for their meals. They were fine men who had chosen a difficult furrow to hoe and were much admired and loved by both Africans and Europeans alike.

There was also in Jumbe a Dutch Reform Church mission consisting of a formidable middle-aged nursing sister and an enormous young male assistant who obviously lived in awe of her. They were, of course, both South African. They ran a hospital, albeit apparently without the benefit of a doctor. The only time we needed their assistance was when my wife developed a severe nose bleed and the good sister gave her a massive injection of a vitamin, I think J, which caused her intense agony and put her in bed for a week.

My least favourite mission was the Anglican mission in Msoro run by the UMCA in the person of an old priest who had been there for years, who clearly should have retired years before and who, equally clearly, had every intention of dying in harness. Msoro was miles away from anywhere and was separated geographically from the rest of the Kunda Valley by a tangle of hills. The trouble was that I got off on the wrong foot with the mission. Having toured with my father, who was concerned entirely with schools, I was interested in them and on my travels would make it my business to call in at the local school and introduce myself to the schoolmaster. They appeared to appreciate my interest and on occasions I could usefully report problems to the Education Department. Most schoolmasters were hardworking and devoted to their calling and their children but there were always a few who were idle, arrogant and venal. On tour in Msoro I came across a distinguished performer in the latter category. I decided on my way back from a bicycle tour of the villages near the chief's headquarters to stop and pay my respects at the large secondary school situated on the outskirts of the chief's village and run, I knew, under the auspices of the UMCA Mission. A secondary school was a rarity. Indeed I guess that it may well have been the only one outside Fort Jimmy in the Eastern Province. I hesitated briefly when I surveyed the substantial range of buildings, but it was after all in my patch and, with the blithe assurance of youth, I marched in, followed by my usual retinue. The retinue including James exhibited, I subsequently admitted to myself, distinct signs of discomfiture. Although it was barely lunchtime the place was deserted. I walked around the classrooms calling out occasionally to announce our presence. Eventually a teenage girl emerged from one of the classrooms looking, I thought, rather coy. She was followed by a youngish schoolmaster. The expressions on the faces of my party indicated clearly that they, like me, suspected the worst. When the schoolmaster got closer it was obvious that he had been drinking. Enquiry elicited that there had been an important local funeral and the children had been let off early to allow the teachers to attend. Funerals in the Valley consisted of a very brief internment followed by an extremely long wake and were, as a result, very popular, except with employers. The teacher recounted this with such insolent relish that I felt my temper beginning to rise. I asked him to bring me the school logbook. This was a book in which a note was made of visits by Education Officers and of other important events in the life of the school. He slouched off in a manner that was clearly intended to, and indeed did, cause me the maximum irritation. What little patience as remained evaporated and with a bellow I told him to run. Such was the concentrated venom in my voice that he did so, returning in very short order with the logbook in which I proceeded to write a report which very accurately reflected my views on the teacher, the school and those who failed apparently to supervise him.

Retribution was quick to arrive. No sooner had I returned to the *boma* than I was summoned to appear before the District Commissioner whom the old priest had made no delay in contacting. He complained that a young District Officer had not only had the impertinence to visit his school without an invitation, or even an appointment, but had then had the nerve to make his teacher run (I could imagine his voice shrilling) to get the logbook, which was reserved for recording congratulatory remarks about the school by eminent visitors (my report had been spread over two pages and so was virtually impossible to erase or remove), and to write in it offensive remarks about the school for all to see. All of this the District Commissioner passed on to me, making it clear that I should regard myself as officially reprimanded. I was subsequently called to see the Provincial Commissioner for the same purpose but it was impossible to miss the twitching of his lips under his moustache. When I reported the incident to my father he confided that the only formal complaint he had ever received came from the same cleric during his time in the Eastern Province.

Another duty for which I was a less enthusiastic volunteer was the auditing of the Native Authority books. Each year the Kunda Native

Authority, like its larger brethren the Chewa and Ngoni, would, during a series of meetings and with the assistance of its District Officer, budget how much money it was going to need to provide the services that were deemed appropriate for its people. Those budgets, when eventually agreed, were delivered to the eagle-eyed accountants in Fort Jameson for approval and, after any necessary amendment (always downwards), were included in the district and provincial and, eventually, departmental allocation of funds.

The budget being approved, and we worked on a total allocation of around £20,000, the day-to-day expenditure was managed by the Kunda Native Authority Treasurer (the son of Chief Jumbe) under the supervision of the District Officer Kunda. So it was that each month the Treasurer would, within a day or so of the end of each month, prepare a trial balance, and each month I would travel down to the Native Authority headquarters and 'audit' the trial balance. The problem was that, having failed to put in an appearance at any of the lectures on the subject at Cambridge, I had never even heard of an animal called a trial balance, let alone having the slightest idea how one set about checking it. Fortunately the Treasurer spoke good English and was kind enough to explain the principle of the thing. He could, had he wanted, have told me a complete fairy tale and thereafter helped himself to the Authority funds. He probably thought that I knew more than I let on and was testing him. He may even have been honest. In any event, armed with this explanation and resisting a strong inclination to burst into tears, I launched myself at the account books that he spread out neatly in a spare office for my inspection. There were, of course, no calculators or even adding machines. The expenditure was all in tiny sums so that there were pages and pages of three-column figures to be added and subtracted. The headquarters building had a tin roof and by midday the heat was intense. There was not even a fan available and the little office in which I laboured was soon like the black hole of Calcutta. Even if the office had been air-conditioned I have no doubt that I would still have sweated with panic, as I struggled to understand what figures I was meant to be comparing with what. My Achilles heel was my elementary mathematics. It was a cruel irony that my first post required me to check, and be responsible for, a local authority annual budget and in circumstances where, at least by reputation, the chances of misappropriation were high. Looking back on it I can only marvel at my temerity in even attempting a task that was so patently fraught with peril and would I suspect give even a qualified Accountant some misgivings. In the event the Kunda

Native Authority accounts seemed to get by without any deficiencies coming to light but that was no thanks to my supervision. I cannot recall, despite the hours I laboured in the heat, ever really understanding what I was meant to be checking against what.

I had less difficulty assisting in the preparation of the annual budget albeit it was an enormously time-consuming and tedious exercise, fraught with political peril. It was, for instance, virtually impossible to reconcile Chief Nsefu's insistence that there should be a new dispensary in his village (as recommended by his son, the Health Councillor) with the reminder from Chief Jumbe that the previous year his demand for a dispensary in his village had been refused against an undertaking that the necessary funds would be allocated this year. On a vote the Chiefs would usually back the Senior Chief but endless negotiations were required to avoid such a confrontation. As a result of sitting out this kind of situation and accepting that the local population did not count time in the same way as we did, I learned to become philosophical about waiting. I travelled usually with at least a rudimentary camping kit, including a very small folding campbed. The kitchen box was stocked as standard with tea, sugar, dried milk and, of course, a tin or two of sausages or the like and a few potatoes so that in the event that the person I had arranged to meet two days hence (pantomime indicating two nights' sleep) at twelve o'clock midday (further pantomime indicating the height of the sun in the sky) failed to arrive on time or at all, I would take up position in the shade and have at least a cup of tea. I was always careful to have a book with me, although gossiping with the Messengers or passers-by, would also help the time pass until either my date turned up or I gave up on him. To be fair the people extended at least equal latitude to me and often, if I had been delayed or, under pressure of events, been unable to keep my appointment, the man I had arranged to meet would be patiently waiting a day or so later.

As part of the same philosophy I learned to adapt my impatient European ways to the more leisurely and forgiving ways of the Kunda. I remember one of my first lessons was given me, I believe, by Chief Mnkanya, who had a large kingdom in the steamy hot middle of the valley. In my first hot season he had done something (I entirely forget what) to incur my wrath. I had made a long and uncomfortable journey in the heat to meet him, so that by the time I reached his village I was pretty well on the boil. As soon as the Land-Rover drew up before his hut I was out and, without waiting for any of the usual formalities, I berated him at length for whatever sin of omission or commission it was that had upset me. He made no attempt to excuse himself but listened impassively to my intemperate outpourings. Eventually, when at last I paused for breath, he quietly said '*Choyamba, Bwana, Mauni*' (First of all, Sir, Greetings.) The implicit quiet rebuke that I should have allowed my bad temper to make me overlook the courtesy of greeting him first was just what was needed to take the wind out of my young sails and to restore my sense of proportion.

I spent days away from the *boma* so that, including the visits to the Game Camp, I actually slept more nights in the Valley than I did at home. On each and every trip I was accompanied by James and usually by Phiri, if there was any chance that I would be away the night. Whether James, or for that matter Phiri, relished racketing around so much, it never occurred to me to enquire. They appeared not to object. I suspect that the frequency of the trips to the Valley had certain compensations, including in James's case, as in mine, the allowance we were given for being away from the *boma* for the day or the night. For James and to a lesser extent for Phiri there was the possibility of some small and not so small trading. It was seldom that James or Phiri would return without smuggling something on to the back of the Land-Rover – something such as vile-smelling dried fish or meat wrapped in leaves, or a sack of vegetables or bananas or tobacco, which were better and certainly cheaper than the equivalent in the Indian stores in Fort Jimmy.

I also had some perks over and above the travelling allowance. One was the samosas that the Indian storeowners would give me whenever they heard I was in Jumbe. Of course, I would always press them to accept payment and, of course, they would refuse. I comforted myself that it would do no harm for them to be preyed upon, bearing in mind the way they took advantage of the local African population. I remember in one store watching an African from the depths of the Valley, to whom the few stores in Jumbe was civilisation with a capital C, admiring some gaudy cotton shirt that was displayed for sale. Eventually he plucked up the courage to ask the storekeeper the price. 'How much you got in your pocket?' the storekeeper demanded, with ill-concealed contempt. The African produced some notes to twice the value of the shirt which he had probably saved for months to accumulate. 'That is the price,' said the storekeeper, extracting the notes with practised ease. I expect I stepped in to redress the balance but undoubtedly this was not an unusual scenario.

Another undoubted advantage of visiting the Valley was the opportunity to shoot guinea fowl, of which there were vast flocks down near

the Luangwa, and I made it a habit always to take the *boma* riot gun
(shotgun) and a supply of cartridges whenever I was likely to be that way.
By coincidence I usually was 'that way' whenever we were likely to be
entertaining. A wild guinea fowl, carefully roasted, made a welcome
alternative to the locally grown and butchered beef. There was nothing
sporting about my shooting which was simply dictated by necessity (if I
was on tour) or greed if I was not. As I travelled around in the
Land-Rover, James and I would keep a sharp look out for guinea fowl
that could often be found in a great flock on the road ahead. Sometimes,
if the canopy was off, I would travel in the back. In that event it was
sometimes possible, if the driver could stop in time and the flock were
slow in reacting, to get in a shot over the cab roof. More usually,
however, I would have to dismount and, running lightly through the
bush, I would try to get around or alongside the flock and get in a shot
before, or as, they took off. The downside to that approach, leaving aside
the difficulty of running in the heat and trying to get in a shot when I
was hot and out of breath, was the ever-present danger of snakes. The
Valley had a splendid variety of snakes including mambas and cobras and
even Gaboon vipers, of which I had a particular dread. Normally the
snakes kept well out of my way, being quick, no doubt, to hear me
coming in plenty of time to get out of sight. What was dangerous was
to move around quietly in bare feet, as did the local Africans who, as
a result, were often bitten. Alternatively it was not clever to run
lightly through the bush in soft-soled shoes with a shotgun in the
high port position and looking keenly into the heavens. Happily,
although I occasionally heard an angry hiss as I took some dozy snake by
surprise, I suffered no greater damage than a sudden increase in my pulse
rate.

In fact, although I shot a considerable number of guinea fowl, as and
when I needed them, I seldom shot anything larger and only when out
on tour and by way of giving in to the entreaties of my African followers.
One of these rare occasions was, however, sufficient to give me a totally
unmerited reputation as a dead shot. Down near the river, on tour in
Chief Malama's area, I had been persuaded that we urgently needed meat
'for the pot'. I accordingly took the *boma* rifle with me in the
Land-Rover one late afternoon and when we saw a herd of impala flitting
through the trees on the side of the road, I got out and, followed by
James at a respectful distance carrying his shotgun, I embarked on an
elaborate stalk which eventually got me close enough to one of the
animals to allow me a shot. I missed and the herd went flying away.

Furious at my miss, after the hot and exhausting stalk, I threw the rifle to my shoulder and, without making any attempt to aim, fired in the general direction of the impalas' fast disappearing white bottoms. Disgusted I turned to walk back to the Land-Rover but James came galloping past me to follow the impala. I was about tell him not to waste his time when he stopped and called excitedly to come and see the impala. Unbelieving, I went to him and found that my ill-tempered shot had hit it neatly behind the head and killed it outright. I would be less than honest if I claimed that I made anything less than a cursory attempt to deny that the shot had been aimed.

James always insisted on taking his shotgun, of which he was rightly extremely proud, whenever we went on tour. My favourite picture of him has him staring into the middle distance with his shotgun across his chest and looking, because he was a fine figure of a man, extremely military, although in fact he was one of the few senior Messengers who was not an ex-Askari. He was, however, distinctly reluctant to be seen to shoot the gun, although he would on occasions lend it to a friend to go and shoot something for him. On one occasion, however, he was bullied and cajoled into trying a shot himself. For this purpose he was installed in the back of the Land-Rover and we set off to find some guinea fowl. After only a short distance a flock obligingly appeared in the road ahead. The driver stopped quietly so as not to disturb the flock, which continued to congregate in the middle of the road. Nothing happened and so I slipped out to investigate. I looked in the back and to my surprise found James, bent double, stalking up the back of the Land-Rover. Why he was at the back of the Land-Rover and not at the front leaning over the cab I had no idea. In any event I whispered to him not to waste time stalking when the birds could not possibly see him and to hurry up and get in a shot over the top of the cab, but by the time he was in position the birds had disappeared round the corner. Although we drove quickly on they had, by the time we got to the corner, disappeared, I suspect to James's secret relief.

The main compensation for the days I spent away from home, which bore most unfairly on my wife, and the long hours I put in was the pleasure I got from what I was doing. This was largely due to the charm and courtesy of the Kunda. I say this despite the political troubles which dominated life in the Valley for most of my time there. I enjoyed the village meetings I attended on tour, particularly when I began to be moderately fluent in Chinyanja. I only occasionally spoke directly to the villagers but, following the example of the Chiefs, would speak quietly

*An entirely unjustified reputation as a shot.*

in Chinyanja which James would repeat in an impressive bellow with such improvements and embellishments as occurred to him. In the process he also put right any grammatical or other errors which would have detracted from my dignity. In reverse he would repeat in slower and more accurate Chinyanja any response from the crowd. This had the purpose of removing any local dialect words that I would not have understood. It also had the advantage, as I became more competent in the language, of giving me time to gather my thoughts while James made his 'translation'.

One of the unfortunate by-products of my touring was that it encouraged my smoking. Although I always had a pipe with me (tucked into the top of my long stockings) I usually ended up smoking the local Gold Leaf filter cigarettes which came in four packs of fifty which cost ten shillings old money. I would travel with hundreds of packets which I used to repay the chickens which were the standard gift that I was given. The cigarettes were pretty mild, certainly compared with the tobacco that the Kunda grew and smoked themselves (either in a pipe or rolled up in newspaper). At the village meetings I usually had a cigarette in my mouth or hand. Apart from their usual function, the cigarettes kept away the flies and also mitigated the smells which were often prevalent in the villages. When I lit up a cigarette, I sometimes offered them around. At that price I could afford to do so. On one splendid occasion, I offered a cigarette to the Chief's Assessor, who had been standing in for the Chief and whom I noticed had been rolling and smoking his own. He took my cigarette and carefully lit it and took an exploratory puff. It obviously made no impression on him, not surprisingly after the raw tobacco he had been smoking rolled up in newspaper. Accordingly he tried a long drag that would have made me dizzy. It obviously still did nothing for him and so, under my disbelieving eyes, he reversed the cigarette and took the burning end into his mouth, drawing the smoke deeply into his mouth.

The manners of the villagers were charming. The men and women would sit on the ground in separate groups. Some of the senior men would sit on small home-made chairs or stools. As we joined the meeting, and again as we left, we were quietly clapped and the women would ululate. If I offered to shake hands (only with the men) they would hold the right wrist with the left hand and at the same time look downwards and make a kind of curtsy. There was nothing subservient about this but merely a mark of respect for a representative of the government. Nicely brought-up young men would do the same to their elders. Occasionally my lighter, which went everywhere with me and which I still keep in distinguished retirement, would fail to light, in which event one of the women would go to the fire which was always burning quietly nearby and roll a few lighted embers onto a piece of bark which she would bring forward and offer on one knee to me or to whichever of the party needed a light. Again it was done naturally and charmingly and I was never conscious of any sense of servility.

Shortly after our arrival there was a general election for a new National Assembly created by the Constitution dreamed up by Reggie Maudling. This Constitution was a compromise over timing. By this stage it had been accepted in principle, following Mr Macmillan's 'wind of change' speech, that there would eventually be majority rule. As the African population had a vast majority over the other races, it followed that universal suffrage would mean an African administration. The issue was when universal suffrage should be introduced. The Federal Government in Salisbury in Southern Rhodesia under Roy Walensky, knowing full well that the first move of an African administration would be to leave the hated Federation, argued that it should be at some period in the distant future. The African politicians unsurprisingly argued vociferously that it should be introduced immediately. Expatriate civil servants, like my father, who had been called in from the Northern Province to set up a new Staff Training College and University to train the young Africans who would be needed as civil servants to run the country following independence, although sympathetic to the African expectations, knew that the practicalities required some time for the necessary infrastructure to be established. Privately they certainly supported the call for Northern Rhodesia to secede from the Federation, which in their view was taking the Northern Rhodesian mineral wealth without giving very much in return.

In any event the compromise produced by Mr Maudling was a Constitution which, in effect, gave the vote to a tiny percentage of the African population but sufficient to give them some representation in the National Assembly while giving political control to the European minority. In practice the country continued to be governed by the expatriate civil servants, albeit that a system of recruiting African civil servants to 'shadow' them was introduced. It was clear that the arrangement could not last very long. Sensing that victory was in sight, the two African parties, UNIP (the United National Independence Party) under Kenneth Kaunda, and ANC (the African National Congress) under Mr Nkumbula, launched campaigns for full adult suffrage and

*A village meeting.*

therefore independence. At the same time they campaigned against each other to establish who was to run the country when, in due course, independence came. I was in no way involved with the election which, indeed, affected so small a proportion of the population that I cannot remember that very much was made of it. I was, however, very much affected by the political campaign and unrest which followed the election.

There had been no history of political activity in the Valley, and certainly no tradition of resentment against white officers, of whom, indeed, in general they appeared to be rather fond. Perhaps this was because until my arrival they had seen so little of them. Unfortunately the UNIP officials who started to move into the area regarded the expatriate civil servants, and District Officer Cadet Goddard in particular, as representing a repressive foreign regime which was holding them in bondage and, but for whom, they would obtain their freedom and so be able to enjoy a land which, but for our depredations, would be flowing, if not with milk and honey, then at least with large quantities of millet beer and maize porridge.

The attitude of the officers who, like me, were in the front line was irritation that the politicians were creating a climate in which it was difficult to deliver the services which the local population badly needed. In the case of the Provincial Administration this meant, I suppose, ensuring that the area enjoyed an orderly and peaceful existence in which local government provided by, or at least in the name of, the Chiefs and central government could give the local population the necessary services it required. The Chiefs were placed in a most invidious position between the District Officers, such as me, who pointed out that if they wanted to continue to receive a stipend from the Government and be provided with Court Clerks and *kapassus*, they would in exchange have to uphold the law, even if this upset the local UNIP officials. These officials on the other hand put the Chiefs under considerable pressure to throw in their lot with the party which would soon be forming the new government and who would not forget Chiefs who had been unsympathetic to their cause.

The ANC were quite strong in the Eastern Province but not in the Kunda valley, which was very obviously dominated by UNIP. Prior to my arrival UNIP had established a strong political infrastructure in the Valley, complete with constituency and district officials and a 'professional' constituency chairman. I had been warned by my predecessor, Bill, that UNIP was operating in the area and I had seen the occasional home-made UNIP sash or armband. I had even seen, but ignored, travelling in the Land-Rover, the occasional UNIP wave (hands held up with fingers extended and waving to illustrate the sun coming up. In other words 'the dawn of freedom') but this had been done in a slightly embarrassed fashion.

My first official brush with UNIP was quick to arrive, on my first tour to Nsefu, in fact. I and my entourage were walking around a village some five miles from the chief's headquarters when we came across a young man with a UNIP sash ostentatiously lolling in a large home-made wooden chair. I had noticed that normally the men, particularly young men, would courteously stand up as I approached or, in the case of women, they would curtsy and clap their hands. I make haste to explain that they did this to senior Africans and not merely to a young cadet. It was patently clear, not only from the young man's attitude but from the embarrassment of my party, that he was making the point that he was not going to acknowledge the presence of an authority of which he was no doubt anxious to see the last. I felt my heart beginning to pound and my breath was a little short as I pondered what to do with a classic case of dumb insolence. I was reluctant to cause a fuss because a young man of about my own age had felt it unnecessary to stand up at my approach and even though, as he well knew, I represented the Government in the area. Clearly there was no law in my book that allowed me to reprimand him. At the same time I was loath to allow the young man to win a victory, which clearly he would have done if I ignored his protest. I had only just arrived in the area and I felt instinctively that it was important to establish my authority at the outset. My objection to his behaviour, as I tried to analyse it, was that it was in breach of the local custom. I accordingly enquired of the Assessor, who was representing the Chief, whether it was customary for young men to loll in chairs when approached by an important visitor who was travelling in the area with the express authority of the Senior Chief. He assured me it was not. 'In that case,' I pronounced, 'I will refer the matter to the Senior Chief who will, I have no doubt, be upset at the discourtesy done to his visitor. One of my Messengers will go with him to tell the Chief what has happened', and in a flash of inspiration I added, 'and he can carry his chair with him.' It was obvious from James's expression that he approved of my solution and he was quick to give the necessary order for the young man to heft the chair onto his head. With the junior Messenger on his bicycle to keep him company, he set off to report to the Chief. I have no doubt that the Messenger was happy to explain to anyone they met why the young man was taking his chair for a walk. That night I received word from the Chief that he was grateful to me for reporting the matter to him 'and particularly for the evidence.'

Gradually the scale of the political activity increased with the arrival of a new and more inflammatory Constituency Chairman who came to visit me. He made no bones about his intention to have me removed and for his party under his leadership to take over the administration of the area. I explained, I trust politely, that my orders prevented my allowing this and that if he or his henchmen broke the law I would have no hesitation in arresting him and them. He obviously paid no attention to my warning and incidents of violence began to mount. There was virtually no ANC presence in the area, or if there was any they wisely kept their heads down, but gangs of youths were recruited to deter anyone who might be opposed to the party and they toured the Valley causing mayhem. Their favourite trick was to set up roadblocks and demand to see the party cards of those passing by. Those who failed to produce them were persuaded to join on payment of a fee. Those who tried to object were manhandled. The victims, although happy to tell their tale, were too frightened by the threat of reprisals (usually having their huts burned down) to want to take the matter further. The Chiefs and their *kapassus* knew exactly what was going on but were themselves too terrified of the consequences to take any action.

Apart from the Chiefs and their elderly *kapassus*, and me and my Messengers on our forays into the Valley, there was no police presence, I thought, until one day, as I was moving around one of the villages in Chief Jumbe's area, I came upon an individual who attracted my attention. I could not put my finger on what it was about him that made me think he was out of place but I made a point of speaking to him and asking him about himself. He was not forthcoming but volunteered to come to my camp that evening to see me, which indeed he did. After making sure we were alone, he admitted that he was a Special Branch officer working under cover in the area who was, he said, following my doings with some interest. He gave me veiled and unspecific warnings about trouble brewing to which, I have to say, I paid little attention. I did, however, take the opportunity when I was next back at the *boma* to visit the police station to ask about the man, whom I half-suspected of being a fraud. I described the man to the Special Branch officer I met who reassured me that I had met Sergeant Mwanza, whose patch was the Kunda Valley. He also warned me, unhelpfully, that trouble, unspecified, was in the wind.

I was indeed aware from my own observations, and from what my Messengers and the friends I was beginning to acquire in the Valley told me, that the new UNIP Chairman was achieving some considerable success in fomenting opposition to the Government. The difficulty was to find the evidence to bring charges against him. It was at this time that I was called out one night, in the middle of my first rainy season, from my camp in Jumbe, to investigate a hut burning further down the Valley in Chief Kakumbi's area. Being young and keen I called out James and another Messenger and set off in the Land-Rover through the rain and the mud to investigate. It was by the merest chance that I slowed on one particular corner just in time to brake before a great chasm, where a river in flood had washed the road away. This was not unusual but when we stopped by the bend, to see what warning we could give to prevent someone else coming to grief, we found that there had been a warning sign but it had been torn down. Obviously some one with a grudge against me had sent word of a hut burning in the expectation that I would go rushing to investigate and charge into the trap.

The road to the game reserves further down the Valley was a great attraction to the UNIP youth gangs. They restricted their roadblocks to the back tracks between villages but on the main road they would usually content themselves with giving the UNIP salute and/or shouting slogans, though on occasions they would throw stones. I had to be sensitive to this as the embryo tourist trade would be very much affected if it got out that it was unsafe to travel in the Valley. Accordingly if, whether by mistake or intention, stones were thrown at my Land-Rover, I and the messengers would give chase. On several occasions the youths would, as they ran, make a point of running under a buffalo bean tree. In fact I think it was a kind of creeper. In any event the beans would, if disturbed by even the slightest breeze such as that created by someone running near by, give off a shower of tiny pores which would set up a quite appalling itch if they got onto the skin. Woe betide any youth whom the Messengers caught after they had run into a cloud of buffalo bean spores.

In the event it was the road which brought matters to a head. James and I and a driver were travelling in the Land-Rover from the *boma* on a day trip. As we came round a bend just before Jumbe, the driver was forced to brake fiercely to avoid a group of men in the road. It took a moment or so for me to realise that we had run into a UNIP roadblock. My immediate instinct was to leap out and try to arrest them (ignoring the fact that we were heavily outnumbered) and indeed I had started to open the door for this purpose when James threw his arms around me and begged me not to try to resist the many hands which were now stretched into the Land-Rover to extract us. I realised that James was entirely right and that discretion was on this occasion the better part of valour and so, trying to pretend I was a willing participant, I allowed myself to be led a few hundred yards into the bush and eventually into a school hall. The hall was already full of villagers both male and female who were being addressed by the new UNIP Chairman. It was hard to believe that the incident was entirely coincidental and I believe that there must have been some advance warning that I would be on the road.

Our escort hustled us to the end of the hall where I was invited to sit at the speaker's table. James and the driver were held to one side. I cannot remember being frightened although, looking back on it, I suppose I should have been. I rather think that I found it difficult to take the situation seriously. In any event the Chairman, apparently reassured by having, as it were, a captive audience, launched into a tirade about my imposing an unacceptable rule on the area to which the majority of the people, as represented by UNIP, strongly objected and ended by assuring me that I was unwelcome in the Valley and suggesting that I should remove myself forthwith from it. This is a summary of a speech which took a very long time to deliver in both the vernacular, so that the audience could enjoy it, and in English, so that I could understand his message. As I sat there listening to his diatribe, I looked idly at the crowd or at least the front few rows. There, in a prominent position, was my old friend Sergeant Mwanza, who obviously had no intention of blowing his cover by coming to my rescue. In the event I rescued myself. I began to detect, as the Chairman rambled on, that he was not only running out of things to say but was beginning to worry what to do with me. In the absence of any threat of violence I was also recovering my nerve and becoming increasingly angry at what was happening. I accordingly rose to my feet and told the assembled multitude that I had been patient long enough and that I was now leaving and that they had not heard the last of the matter, whereupon I marched briskly towards the door, followed closely by James and the driver. To my relief the crowd parted before us and we were allowed to return unmolested to our Land-Rover.

Back in the *boma* I reported the matter to the District Commissioner and the Police and the next day a punitive expedition of two lorry loads of Police in riot kit was dispatched at crack of dawn to apprehend the culprits. James and I travelled with them to identify our attackers. We made a sweep through the village and every last man jack of the roadblock crew were arrested and taken back to Fort Jameson where they were sentenced to longish terms in jail. James was marvellous at remembering exactly and precisely who was to blame and, if he gave them a cuff as they were thrown up into the lorry, I found it difficult to blame him. Of the Chairman there was needless to say no sign. He obviously knew that retribution was to be expected and found urgent business that required him to leave the area that night.

Although the removal of the visitation by the Police did a lot to quieten things down, I did not take any pride in having to call for assistance from outside the Valley and I determined to be more active in preserving law and order. The first thing I did was to persuade the Chiefs to sack at least one of their elderly *kapassus* and to recruit some younger men in their place. Stage two was to get them to agree that the new *kapassus* should be posted turn and turn about at the Native Authority Headquarters in Jumbe where I stayed on a regular basis in the purpose-built rest house there. My plan was to have a small group of active men who could reinforce my Messengers if there was any trouble. That is to overlook my touring cook, Phiri, who, entirely unasked and entirely unofficially, took to bringing a ferocious-looking knobkerrie on tour with him and appointing himself as my night watchman as well as cook. He also, on one occasion when we made a dawn raid on a village to try to catch some evildoer, joined in the sweep. The first I knew of it was when I turned round and to my horror found him, complete with the little pillbox hat that completed his cook's uniform, padding along a few feet behind me smiling beatifically and with his fearsome club over his shoulder. Reluctantly I had to insist that in future he restricted his activities to his cooking pots and his night-time watch.

Towards the end of the rains there was another upset, this time in Chief Malama's area. The District Commissioner received a strange letter, signed by my old friend the Chairman, announcing that on behalf of the people of the area he was declaring independence. I supposed he calculated that he was safe to make this gesture as no one in their right mind would try to visit the area during the rains when the road which ran along the bank of the Luangwa was flooded for most of the rainy period. I was inclined to be relaxed about the situation. The idea of Chief Malama's six scruffy villages declaring independence ahead of the rest of the country was more of a joke than a challenge to the Government. The District Commissioner, however, no doubt correctly, felt that we could not afford to ignore the matter and I contemplated, with considerable misgivings, the possibility of walking in. It was James who remembered

*A punitive expedition.*

that there used to be a track in over the hills in Chief Msoro's area which, even if it did not get us right into Malama's village, would certainly give us a far shorter walk than along the Luangwa. Obviously we needed some show of force and so I took six messengers as well as James, a Messenger driver and, of course, Phiri. Even a long wheelbase Land-Rover would not carry that number and so we also took the *boma* Vanette.

It was a nightmare journey which took some twelve hours, as I recall. The first part of the journey along the Great East Road and then along the well-used track to Msoro was no trouble. Even the track over the hills was possible, if bumpy. The real trouble started in the flat land beyond the hills which was a flood plain and at that time of the year inundated with water. The Land-Rover struggled but the Vanette was completely overwhelmed. At times I was close to abandoning the expedition but we struggled on, manhandling the Vanette which, for most of the way, we towed from the Land-Rover. We arrived late at night muddy and exhausted and camped in the playground of the local school. Obviously news of our arrival had gone ahead of us and we went to sleep with the sound of drumming coming from the Chief's village nearby. The next morning I received word that the Chairman had been very shaken by our unexpected arrival and had sent out word around the villages during the night to summon the faithful to join him. As the sun rose, the drumming started up again and as I sat in a chair and at a table commandeered from the school to eat my breakfast, I confess to a distinctly queasy feeling in the pit of my stomach as I waited for events to unfold. I did not have long to wait. The noise of many voices rose above the sound of the drums and got nearer and then a crowd of about 100-strong, led by the Chairman (an insignificant little man to look at), some brandishing sticks and some spears, marched onto the playground which was a sandy area enclosed by bush. They advanced towards me. The Messengers who had been standing behind me moved to form a semi-circle between me and the crowd. Although the Messengers were a tough bunch, all of them, with the exception of James, ex-soldiers, they were unarmed except for their police truncheons which would have been of little use if things got out of hand against such a crowd.

Both at the time and looking back, I never cease to be amazed at the loyalty and courage of the Messengers. They knew perfectly well that the chances were that an African government was a distinct possibility in the near future, in which event expatriate officers such as myself would disappear back to England. They had no such escape route and would be left to the mercies of their countrymen who might, for all they knew, be in a mood to inflict reprisals. Despite this, the Messengers on this occasion, as on many other occasions, were prepared to accept considerable risks to uphold the law and protect their European officers. I like to think that this may have been a reflection of the generosity of African people who seem to be prepared to forgive the most grave injustices and injuries done to them, as in South Africa, without seeking to inflict revenge when in a position to do so. Perhaps the Messengers and others such as Phiri who were prepared to stand up to UNIP had a confidence, which I confess I would have found hard to share in their circumstances, that their countrymen would not hold it against them that they had done what they were obliged to do. I never heard that any of our people were ever victimised after independence.

However, no such considerations would have prevented the crowd chopping all of us up had they had a mind to do so. Happily they did not seem to have a mind to do so although that was not immediately apparent. There was a great deal of shouting and chanting (most of which, perhaps fortunately, I could not understand. I understood or guessed enough to know that in summary they were saying 'Go home, District Officer Cadet Goddard. We don't want you here!' There was a great deal of surging against the line of Messengers and occasionally James, who had remained standing by my side when the others went forward, went forward to lend a hand but the Messengers remained calm, and behaved with remarkable restraint under considerable provocation, and the line held.

I remained sitting in the shade of a small tree not because of any coolness of nerve but because I could not think of anything else to do. This stand-off lasted the best part of an hour and I called for Phiri, who was lurking protectively near by, to bring me another cup of tea. Happily his club was not in evidence. The sun rose and it got hotter and eventually the shouting started to die away so that eventually I called out, and James repeated with an impressive bellow, that I was not prepared to talk to a crowd but that I would be prepared to talk to a small deputation. This elicited another paroxysm of shouting but my friend the Chairman, who was in the front and had been leading them, turned and gestured to his followers to be silent and, with five or six others, came forward and the Messengers let them through until they stood before me.

It was getting really very hot and I was glad of my shade, small though it was, as the sun rose to its zenith. Courteously, as I thought, I suggested that they should sit down but apparently this was not a good idea because, as the deputation told me, it would have meant that they, the people's proper representatives, would have had to sit at my feet like slaves (as they put it) and unfortunately (or fortunately as it turned out) the school only boasted one chair on which I was sitting and on which it was clear I had every intention of continuing to sit. In vain did I point out to them that the day was hot and that it was tiring to stand and that it would be much more sensible for them to sit, admittedly near my feet, in the shade. The more I tried to persuade them the more adamant they were that they would stand. It seems incredible looking back but this argument as to whether the deputation should sit in the shade or stand in the sun lasted for another hour or so. Meanwhile the crowd had not only stopped shouting but had instead started to drift away, as crowds will if nothing exciting is happening, and the deputation showed signs of wanting to follow them. Then things changed and the Messengers, who had been keeping the crowd back, instead turned and, as the deputation tried to leave, politely but firmly restrained them. Eventually when most of the crowd had retreated, the deputation, seeing that the game was up, sank gratefully to the ground and I allowed them (with the exception of the Chairman) to go back to their villages with a homily about the dangers of listening to UNIP officials. My friend, the Chairman, I took into custody. He showed no resentment and indeed, at James's suggestion, played an active part in helping the tired Messengers and me to pack the vehicles and then manhandle them through the mud on the way back to the *boma*. There the Resident Magistrate took a dim view of his behaviour and he was sent off to prison for some time.

With the Chairman removed and with the new force of *kapassus* at the Native Authority headquarters there were no further major troubles, but there were more local confrontations as I continued to tour around the villages. I became adept at judging when I could in effect stare an angry gathering down or better still make them laugh or when it was better to beat a hasty retreat, usually when they had been drinking. In virtually every case it was the young men who were the trouble. It was clear that it was at least as much their frustration with their lives as political commitment that led them to be such a nuisance. The trouble was that there was nothing for them in the Valley, I argued, so that unless they were prepared to remain as subsistence farmers with virtually no cash income, which increasingly they were not prepared to contemplate, the only solution was for them to emigrate to the Copper Belt in Northern Rhodesia or the coal mines in Southern Rhodesia and try to earn enough to retire to their villages. This was not good for them nor was it good for their villages and it was pretty dire for the District Officer on whom they turned to take out their anger.

It was against that background that I had the bright idea of setting up a youth scheme. I would ask the Chiefs to volunteer their six naughtiest young men for three months and I would provide them with a rudimentary uniform and food and lodging and training in bricklaying, thatching and carpentry. The advantage to the young men was that it would give them trades which would enable them to earn a living and remain in the area. The advantage to the Government, as the Chiefs with whom I discussed it were quick to see, was that it would keep the young men in the villages and provide the means and incentive to the more affluent of their subjects to improve their houses. For me there was the advantage that it would keep thirty-six potential stone throwers out of my way for a while.

I chewed the practicalities of the scheme over for some time. It was comparatively easy to recruit the tradesmen to teach the skills and to pay them as Native Authority employees. The funds for this purpose and for the provision of uniforms (purchased at a huge discount from the Indian stores in Jumbe) and the provision of equipment and materials (their first project was to build themselves some dormitories; until they were completed they could easily build themselves grass shelters) came from the Native Authority. To disguise this expenditure and with the cooperation of the Treasurer, we robbed money allocated for the maintenance of the roads, which anyway, as I argued, would be washed away by the rains. I was, of course, spared the restraints that would even then have been imposed had the exercise been proposed in this country, such as Planning Consent or Health and Safety approvals or insurance or any of the other considerations which prevent any but the most determined of adults proposing anything as dangerous for children as a walk in the park.

What was difficult was finding someone to undertake the day-to-day supervision and discipline of the enterprise. Obviously I could not tie myself up for the three months that was required and indeed I was not really sure exactly what kind of person or persons I needed. In the event, as so often happens, the hour produced the man in the shape, in fact, of two men. One was a Volunteer for Service Overseas, an incredibly insouciant young man, I suppose of about eighteen, just out of Public School, who by some extraordinary good luck for me, had found his way to the *boma* apparently without any clear idea what he was meant to be doing. How or why he was there I had and have not the slightest idea, nor in the circumstances did I care; I was only grateful that a beneficent providence had provided me with just the kind of confident young man with powers of leadership, as I assumed, who would allow himself to be deposited in the Kunda Valley to oversee the self-improvement of thirty-six of the area's most belligerent young men. He seemed perfectly happy with my proposition that he should be seconded to me for some months and live on his own in the Valley. The District Commissioner also approved the placement which relieved him I, suspect, of having to find something else for him to do.

Whatever worries I may have felt about my new recruit's safety, and I confess I cannot recall many, were calmed by the further recruit who fell into my hands. He was an African Police Inspector whom I met at the Katete Agricultural Show. This was an annual show held in Katete, a substation of Fort Jameson, which, being the only event of its kind in the province, was visited by most of the European officers in the province and my wife and I attended at the invitation of friends of ours who had recently been posted there. While watching the Police band putting on a display, I fell into conversation with the Inspector who was, I think, suspended from duty following an accident or illness, and he was bemoaning the fact that he was getting bored with nothing to do. I mentioned, more in hope than expectation, that I just happened to be about to start a youth scheme in the Kunda Valley and could do with the assistance of someone just like him. To my delighted amazement he immediately volunteered that it was just the kind of thing that he was looking for. Both of us agreed that it might be unfair to trouble his superiors with the matter, in case they worried about the advisability of a Policeman, and one of the few African inspectors to boot, being attached to an unofficial scheme dreamed up by a very new cadet.

The enormous advantage of these two volunteers was that they would be paid for by some other organisation, although I suspect that I may have been able to offer some assistance with their food. And so it was that the Kunda Valley Youth Training Scheme came into being. The thirty-six young men duly appeared, at the bidding of their various Chiefs, looking rather apprehensive, as they had every right to be, at Masumba. Masumba was the perfect place for the enterprise; it was in the geographical centre of the Valley and on the main road to the game reserves. It was in the tribal area of Chief Mnkanya, who was a sensible unassuming little man, so that neither Chief Jumbe nor Chief Nsefu would feel slighted, as they would have done had the camp been situated in the area of the other. It was flat land so that it was easy to build on and even more importantly, so far as the boys were concerned, it was not difficult to create a football pitch. We had an unexpected bonus in that it appeared that our young VSO had been to a public school which unusually played football rather than rugby and was furthermore quite a distinguished player so that he gained immediate kudos as being able to coach the boys in the finer points of the game. Finally it had a grove of enormous baobab trees beneath whose branches I built a large grass fence and the usual offices so that I could hold meetings and easily and comfortably spend the night whenever I was in the area. Chief Mnkanya put in an appearance at the opening ceremony when I introduced the instructors and managers to their charges and issued them with rudimentary uniforms of khaki shorts and different coloured singlets depending on their chief, and left them to it.

Needless to say over the next few months I made it my business to find things to do and people to see in the Mnkanya area so that I had an excuse to visit the camp. I had two unnerving experiences there. They both occurred during the hottest part of the dry season when the Kunda sensibly went into what I can only describe as a state of suspended animation when they spent most of the day lolling in the shade. They had every excuse for doing so as the temperature in the Valley was horrendous, with no breath of wind to cool things down and with a heat haze lying over the whole area. Only keen young cadets were silly enough to think it necessary to drive down to the Valley in the heat of the day. The movement of the Land-Rover with the front vent and windows wide open created a breeze that made it just about bearable to sit squashed into the front seat of the vehicle with James's substantial bulk between me and the driver. On this day one of my favourite messengers, Chicomeni Banda, was driving for me. He was about my age, an ex-Askari who had seen action, I believe in Malaya. He was an inch or so shorter than my five foot nine, with incredibly bandy legs which made him roll as he walked, but with the most powerful torso of anyone I have ever seen. He was not very clever and his English was poor but he was willing and always cheerful and I liked having him with me on tour. As we arrived at Masumba, I waited for a few moments to allow the cloud of red dust that always billowed forward over the Land-Rover as we halted to disperse before getting out. It was frighteningly hot. As I got out, the heat descended on me like a cloud of steam. I had a momentary feeling of panic that I could not breathe or function. Chicomeni had got out before me and had immediately taken off his heavy blue tunic and bush hat, leaving him in his service issue vest, before going off, I

*Boys in training at Masumba.*

presumed, for a drink of water. A few moments later there was a cry and when I went to investigate I found Chicomeni collapsed on the ground. We tried to get him up but his body was rigid as if paralysed. I considered the possibility of a heart attack or something similar (not that I knew the symptoms) but I guessed he was too young and fit for that and it occurred to me that it might be heat stroke, in which event I reasoned the right thing was to get his temperature down. I called for water which we poured and sponged over him and, sure enough, in a little while his enormous muscles, which appeared to be in spasm, began to relax and gradually he came to and soon afterwards was able to travel back to the *boma* with me driving.

The second unpleasant experience occurred when I was spending the night at Masumba. I went to bed on my own in the grass enclosure on a low stretcher bed which I always used on tour and which was only a couple of inches above the ground. I slept in the open to get what breeze was available. I did not bother with a mosquito net and I lay in my underpants on top of the bedding. There was an oil lamp on a pole some distance away which gave some slight illumination. The Messengers and Phiri were also some distance away, I guessed eating with the camp staff. The VSO had gone off to his own roost. It was very quiet and I drifted off to sleep. Something woke me and I looked around me. To my horror, silhouetted against the light from the oil lamp, at the foot of my bed was a large snake looking down at me. I lay frozen with horror while I considered what to do. Should I lie still and hope the snake would lose interest in me and go on about his business? But what if it decided to investigate me a little closer and if I gave an involuntary movement would he not strike? The very thought of having the reptile any closer than he already was galvanised me into activity and I leaped backwards from the bed with a vigour that only terror can inspire, at the same time uttering what I intended to be a shout but was more of a scream. In any event it had the desired effect, as Phiri and the Messengers came running to my assistance at the same time as the snake made off in the other direction. I confess that my enthusiasm for camping at Masumba waned for some time.

CHAPTER 5

# The second year

PARAMOUNT CHIEF NSEFU died at the beginning of my second year with the Kunda. I was very fond of the old gentleman and I missed his old-world charm and courtesy. Whether his reputation as a poisoner was merited or not, I do not know, but certainly there was some steel under his gentle manner and he was quite prepared to stand up to me if he disagreed with me. Even more importantly, and unusually, he was prepared to back me, if he agreed to do so, despite the heavy pressure I was aware he came under from the politicians. When he fell ill, the Chief was taken, not to the usual Government hospital, but to the Seventh Day Adventist Hospital, a few miles out of Fort Jameson, where a considerable number of his tribe soon gathered, camping out in the hospital gardens. I recognised among them his usual entourage, including his Assessors and his senior *kapassus*, and his son Mr Chulu, the Councillor. There was also a team of women of various ages, whom I took to be his wives.

I used to drive out of an evening to see the Chief who was obviously dying, as the doctors confirmed. Mr Chulu took the opportunity to have a quiet word with me, on one of these visits, to ask me to promise to come to the hospital immediately the end came and to ensure that the body was taken back to the Valley, where the funeral was to take place according to tribal custom. Accordingly I made a point of remaining at my desk in the *boma* for the next few days and when the word came, in the early evening just as I was relaxing with a beer, that the Chief had died, I went straight out to the hospital. I had arranged to take the Land-Rover home with me to cover just such an eventuality. I had no Messenger or driver so I drove myself. When I turned off the road to enter the grounds of the hospital, I became aware of the most appalling wailing, which I could see emanated from the crowd of followers, which appeared to have grown since my last visit. Trying to block my mind to the din, I forced my way through the crowd and into the hospital where a harassed doctor shouted at me, above the noise, to hurry and remove the body as the followers were threatening to invade the hospital, and anyway the noise was making it impossible for the hospital to function.

I shouted back to ask if there was an ambulance he could lend me. He shook his head.

'Or at least a coffin?'

He shook his head again. I would have to get that from the *boma*.

'Try PWD,' he shouted, trying to be helpful, but obviously desperate for me to remove his problem. Back in the ward the doctor helped to wrap the corpse in some sheets, and then the orderlies carried the body, as I led the way through the crowd to my Land-Rover. I lowered the tailgate (fortunately the canvas cover was in place over the back of the vehicle, as it was still the rainy season) and the body was laid as reverently as possible on the metal floor. The wailing reached a crescendo, perhaps fortunately, as there then ensued a desperate struggle among the wives and followers to get on the Land-Rover for the honour of escorting the Chief on his final journey. Scant regard seemed to be paid to the body lying on the floor of the vehicle, as they struggled for position. I comforted myself with the thought that the Chief was past feeling the unheeding feet that trampled on him. Eventually, with Mr Chulu in front with me and with a dozen or so of what appeared to be the best wailers in the back, I headed the Land-Rover back to Fort Jameson, leaving the remainder of the crowd to find their way back to the Valley for the funeral.

By the time I drove my noisy cargo into Fort Jimmy it was getting towards bedtime. I headed to the *boma* and left word with the duty Messenger to call out a Messenger driver to take over from me when I got back, which I promised to do in half an hour, to take the Land-Rover and its cargo straight on down to the Valley for the funeral. Having made that arrangement I then set off to find a coffin. The duty Messenger had agreed that PWD (Public Works Department) had a stock of coffins but he did not know which department. The PWD, like the Hydra, had many heads – roads, vehicle maintenance, house building and repairs and a host of others – and I had not the slightest idea which department was responsible, at ten o'clock at night, for the issue of coffins. The noise from the back of the Land-Rover made it difficult to think, as I tried in vain to imagine to what department the bureaucratic mind would think to allocate the manufacture and storage of coffins. Feeling rather like the proverbial cat with a can attached to its tail, I set off around the European housing estates to find the man who would give me a coffin. I tried the District Commissioner who was just getting into bed. He did not know and was, I detected, not very sympathetic to my predicament.

I went home, both to explain my delay in returning and to ask if my wife had any ideas about coffins. She was sympathetic but had no idea where I could find a coffin but suggested our nice Scots neighbour, who was in PWD albeit Vehicle Maintenance. I left the Land-Rover, with its wailers in good voice, in my drive, trying to close my mind to what the neighbours thought, while I went across the road and banged on my Scottish neighbour's door. He was desperate to be helpful, but after long cogitation had to admit that he didn't know himself but he did know a man who might. I set off again and visited no fewer than five other addresses, bringing a noisy touch of the macabre to most areas of the European township before eventually, around midnight, finding another cheerful little Scotsman, who happily volunteered that he would be happy to provide me with a coffin provided he had one of the right size. I tried to remember the Chief's size but patently my explanation that he was 'quite small but a bit bigger than you but not quite as tall as I am' was not very helpful and eventually, at his suggestion, we pulled the corpse out from under the feet of the wailers and laid it out on his drive where he measured it. The rest of it, following my rescuer to the PWD stores in town where he kept an impressive array of coffins and placing the chief in one, was child's play. I confess that when the Messenger driver eventually took over from me to take the body and its chorus to the Valley, I felt that a considerable weight had been lifted from my shoulders.

I think it was James who advised against attending the funeral. From the account that I subsequently received of the violently emotional scenes at the graveside, which a European would have found distasteful, I was glad that I had taken his advice. After a decent interval the question of a successor to the Paramount Chief arose. Although very much affected by the choice, particularly as the political process towards independence was accelerating, neither I, nor the *boma*, had any say, or at least any direct say, whom the successor should be. I personally would have been delighted had Mr Chulu, the Chief's eldest son, been appointed, but unhappily the Kunda were a matrilineal tribe rather than patrilineal like the Ngoni and the Southern African tribes such as the Zulus from whom they were descended. The simplistic summary of the difference between the two systems was, and as far as I know still is, that in a patrilineal system the children of the marriage belong to the bridegroom's family. As new recruits to the family or tribe are a valuable resource as potential warriors, if male, or workers and the mothers of warriors, if female, the bridegroom and his family have to pay handsomely, in the form of cows or whatever, for that privilege. Under a matrilineal system, on the other hand, the children belong to the mother's family, which enormously discounts the value of the bride, as she brings only herself to the bridegroom and his family. As a result, in my time the going rate for a Kunda bride was a chicken or two, a fact which the Messengers who travelled regularly to the Valley with me were quick to discover.

The implications of the matrilineal system could lead to all kinds of strange results, as in the choice of a successor to the chief. Offensive though we may find it, the fact is that women, certainly in my time in Africa, had very few rights and were to all intents and purposes chattels. I imagine that the historical reason for that was that, in an era when one's very existence depended on physical prowess as a hunter or warrior, it was impossible for a woman to exist except under a man's protection. Before we become too patronising, it is instructive to remember that in civilised England it was not until the Married Woman's Property Act of 1866 that women could hold property in their own name and that until that time any property to which a woman was entitled belonged in law to her father, trustees or husband. Under the matrilineal system a child did not belong to his or her father and could not belong to his mother (because she could not in effect own anything) and so the child was owned by the woman's senior male relative on her mother's side. This would be her mother's senior brother or, in the absence of any uncles, her own brothers in descending order of age. Inheritance operated in the opposite direction so that it was not a man's son who inherited (there was, of course, no question of a woman inheriting) but his senior sister's eldest son. I have no doubt that there were subtleties and exceptions to this depending, I guess, on the personalities involved, but they did not appear to have operated in this case and the successor, according to Kunda tribal law, to become the paramount chief of the Kunda was a man in his forties, who lived in the Copper Belt and whom no one had seen for many years.

Although I had no role to play in the selection process, the Kunda had no hesitation in seeking my assistance with the collection and installation of the new Chief. Thus it was that a few weeks later my wife and I set off in the Land-Rover with a driver and a representative from the Kunda to collect the new Paramount Chief designate. I believe that James did not accompany us; he would have had to sit in the dust in the back, and anyway we had our own agenda. My father had been diagnosed with cancer. They had operated, apparently successfully, but we were anxious to spend some time with him and we also planned to buy ourselves a motor car.

We started off in the Copper Belt to collect the new Chief. We eventually found him, not without difficulty, outside a hut in one of the mine townships. He was not particularly prepossessing – of medium height, slightly built and with his hair long on top and brushed *en brosse* I believe it is called, so that it stood on end rather than lying flat. He had rather protuberant eyes which, with the hair piled on top, gave him a rather pop-eyed appearance. There was not much formality. The Chief had, of course, long since heard that the old Chief was ill and then that he had died, leaving him as the heir. I introduced myself and congratulated him on his elevation to become the father of the tribe. The Kunda representative was rather more fulsome in his respects. We then loaded the new Chief, and a small suitcase, onto the Land-Rover, leaving his goods and chattels and his wife or wives to follow him later. We then returned to Lusaka, on wonderful metalled roads – such a joy after hammering over corrugated earth roads – where we were dropped off to collect our first car, leaving the Land-Rover to take the new Chief back to the Eastern province.

The new car (second-hand, of course, purchased with the aid of a second Government loan) was a VW Beetle, which in due course we drove back in triumph to Fort Jameson in a cloud of red dust over the corrugated earth surface of the Great East Road, which our new vehicle, we congratulated ourselves, seemed to take in its stride. It really was the most excellent motor car which, despite the most appalling misuse over a vast number of miles, never let us down. No longer did my wife have to rely on friends to get to work or to go to the Indian stores. It made a huge difference to our lives, as only those who have been without their own transport will appreciate.

There was, however, a further reason for our launching into the purchase of a car, namely the imminent arrival on holiday of my mother-in-law and, overlapping with her, my brother for part of his long vacation from Oxford. In addition to our six months' home leave every two and a half years (after a first tour of three years) we were also entitled to some weeks' local leave (I forget how many) which, with the permission of the District Commissioner, I could take when convenient (his convenience not mine, of course). That leave had to be taken locally, although the practicalities prevented one going back to Europe in any case. I had saved up my local leave, which I confess was no hardship as I found the work so exciting that I could hardly bear to miss a day. In any event we splurged our leave on travelling as far as we could, while family were with us, in our new car. We visited the Victoria Falls, via the newly-built Kariba dam, on one long trip and Lake Nyasa on another. Of course we also visited the Nsefu Game Reserve where I had constructed my own grass enclosure and huts on a bluff overlooking the camp.

I had also been planning for some time to go on a walking tour and the visit of my brother was an obvious opportunity to do so. Not long before, walking was the only way of getting around the more isolated villages but the tour on foot had become rare, largely because organising and embarking on a walking tour was time-consuming and difficult to justify in relation to one's other duties, unless one had a good reason for it. In my case I had, I thought, a very good reason, namely to reconnoitre a route for a Land-Rover track over the hills between Masumba, in Chief Mnkanya's area, and Chief Malama's villages. The journey through the mud during the rains was still fresh in my memory. By 'walking' tour I mean one where I stayed out for several nights taking my camping gear and food with me (as opposed to being deposited at a central point where I stayed for several days, walking out for the day, which I often did). These tours required taking several days' food and water and camping gear, not only for the District Officer, but also for the Messengers, and involved hiring porters to carry the gear. General orders had detailed instructions as to the number of porters to which a Provincial Commissioner and District Commissioner and a District Officer were entitled. The entitlements were fairly lavish and I doubt whether I was in any danger of exceeding even a cadet's entitlement, when I dispatched a couple of Messengers to accumulate the necessary manpower for a three-day walking tour. Finding the necessary recruits was easy, as paid work was in short supply in the Valley, and carrying heavy loads long distances in the heat was something every villager did on a regular basis, particularly if he was short of wives to carry the loads for him. Everything went on the head, if at all possible, and I used to marvel at the extraordinary items that were balanced there, apparently without difficulty, or indeed thought, sometimes directly on the head, sometimes on a little mat or cloth. Undoubtedly it was this custom of carrying things on their heads which gave the people, both male and female, such wonderful deportment. In the same way the hoeing and pounding of maize with large poles in huge wooden mortars gave the women their beautiful shoulders and upper arms.

In any event my brother and I, and James and a couple of other Messengers, and Phiri, of course, duly set off, early one morning, at the head of a dozen or so carriers into the hills behind Mnkanya, heading towards the fiefdom of my old friend Chief Malama. Although we had chosen a cool time of the year and my brother and I were both pretty

*My mother-in-law on tour at the District Officer's camp at Nsefu with Phiri and James in attendance.*

fit, it was hard work. For most of the way there was no track to follow
and no clear indication of what was the best route to take, as we pushed
our way through the elephant grass and between the scrubby little trees.
We stopped at regular intervals to give the carriers a few minutes' rest,
although they gave no sign of being distressed and indeed chatted to each
other without pause. They appeared to have the knack of throwing their
voices, so that although there was a considerable distance between the
front and rear of the single file in which they travelled, there seemed to
be no difficulty in getting remarks and, by the laughter, jokes from the
back to the front of the line and vice versa.

I cannot remember that I had a map to follow, and indeed even if I
had it would have been virtually impossible to map read, bearing in mind
that there were no distinguishing features to recognise but just mile after
mile of entirely featureless scrub-covered hills shimmering in the heat.
Nor indeed did I have a compass, or if I carried one I cannot
remembering using it, preferring instead to rely on the sense of direction
of the Messengers and the carriers, some of the latter having professed to
having travelled the route before. If they had, they had obviously taken
different routes, as I recall several disagreements as to which way to go.
We carried plenty of water with us (in the usual canvas bags which made
the water taste strongly of . . . canvas) which was just as well, as we found
no water on the way. We camped in the open as soon as it started to get
dark. We carried sleeping bags but no campbeds or tents and we slept
round the fire with the Messengers and Phiri with the unforgettable smell
of wood smoke in the air. I woke several times during the night and there
seemed always to be someone awake, smoking and gossiping and making
up the fire. The carriers had their own fire to sleep by. We gradually
woke by common consent with the first light of dawn. It was cold and
we all, European and African alike, huddled companionably round the
fire with blankets or sleeping bags over our shoulders, sipping tea and
delaying as long as possible the moment when we needed to attend to
the business of the day.

The Messengers were as usual anxious that I should shoot something
for the pot, and I had brought along the *boma* rifle and shotgun for that
purpose, but although we surprised a magnificent kudu in a thicket, he
had also surprised us and there was, to my relief, no possibility of a shot.
Towards the end of the trip I did manage to shoot some guinea fowl.
We camped the second night in a dried river-bed. I was inspired to try
to cook one of the guinea fowl in a hole in the sand in the approved
aborigine fashion, which was a disaster. The next morning Phiri made

some bread in a saucepan in a hole in the sand which was delicious. In due course we reached Malama's villages where we were to be collected by the Land-Rover. The trip had been fun and had the useful purpose of proving that there was a way over the hills, at least on foot, but although it would be possible to make a Land-Rover track, it would be a major enterprise and beyond my capabilities.

It was, I think on a different occasion, while waiting in Malama's village for some hours, that I had the opportunity to study two of his wives going about their chores. I was given a chair, which I set up in the shade of a hut, and pretended to read. After a while everyone forgot I was there, leaving me free to watch the village unobtrusively from under the brim of my hat. The two wives were about the same age and with a baby each of about the same age. They were obviously good friends and worked happily together as a team, pounding maize and sweeping the area around the cluster of huts that constituted the Malama family home. The babies spent part of their time slung on the girls' backs and part of the time slung on the front suckling. The babies were, however, old enough to be unslung from time to time to lie and chuckle to themselves on a cloth on the sandy ground until they grew restive, in which case the nearest girl would scoop him, or perhaps it was her, up and suckle him or sling him on her back. This happened several times over the several hours that I sat there and I became intrigued to determine which baby belonged to which mother. I watched carefully to see which mother suckled which child. At the end of my observation I could still not make up my mind which was which and I was forced to the conclusion that their relationship was so close that although obviously the mothers and babies knew who belonged to whom, for all practical purposes it did not matter. There must, I pondered, be considerable advantages in such an arrangement.

We were sorry to see our relatives depart but there was plenty to keep us occupied and I was away on tour a great deal trying to keep on top of the political situation and to implement some constructive policies. The Masumba scheme was popular and undoubtedly contributed to a period of comparative calm. I also had the advantage that with my friend the UNIP Chairman out of the way, I was more established than the man who was sent to replace him and he apparently decided, for a period, that discretion was the better part of valour. In August 1963 it was announced that there was to be a new constitution, and new elections, with a much wider electorate than before, were to be held in January the next year. It was obvious that this would result in an African

MALAMBO CONSTITUEN

JUMBE BRANCH,
BOX 134,
FORT JAMESON.

8/4/63

Cadet GODARD
FORT JAMESON.

1. WE Indegenous people of this free land of Akunda would no longer come to a compromise with you. We are completely UNITED against your continuation as A KUNDA NATIVE AUTHORITY CADET.

2. As already told on the 8th of this month of April,1963 that you had to go back to Fort Jameson and no more here,it was a fact and we shall stick to that.We mean what we mean and what the free people of the HOLY KUNDA VALLEY MEAN.

3. We shall protest to any means of Force which you will try to implement as breakdown our strong feelings against you.We have masttered this in strongest terms and principles.

4. We shall however,like to have another or say a new D.O Kunda Native Authority,who will then have to for work in harmony with the free sinless people of this end.

5. There will be no more any round table talks in as to find means of settling this matter.A new man with a human spirit,will we hope do us better than you.

6. We again pointing out this in clear terms that,the summons issued to Councillor J.R.Zimba and driver E.Sakala have met the strongest protest from the mass of people in the Kunda Valley.

7. We here ask you to free those two innocent people.If there will be any case against these two gentlemen,we shall be very glad as to transfare it to the Akunda people here.We are ready to face any problems which affects the Kunda Native Authority Lorry.

8. Do not take this as a silly and joking matter as you have been always putting it.We do not like your principles.

      A W A Y  W I T H  YOUR I N J U S T I C E.

      Yours in it

      BRANCH CHAIRMAN.

cc The Provincial Commissioner, F.Jameson,
" The District Commissioner "
" The Regional Secretary Box 166 F.Jameson.
" Acting Senior Chief Nsefu.

110

majority. To reflect this, the Central African Federation was dissolved. None of the Africans and few of the expatriate civil servants regretted its passing. One immediate result of the announcement of the new elections was the need to register the voters, in effect the total resident population, including women. The process of registration was carried out by the Court Clerks working from the tax lists and the Messengers and I were heavily involved trying to ensure that there was no skulduggery. It was an obvious temptation for the local UNIP gangs to try to prevent their political opponents of the ANC being registered to vote by intimidating them or the Registration Officer or both. There was, in fact, very little trouble in the Valley where there was overwhelming support for UNIP and I rather enjoyed attending the registration meetings which were held in the villages. The villagers took the process of registering to vote very seriously and as the majority of the village population was female (because the majority of the able-bodied male population were away in the Copper Belt) they dressed in their best for the occasion so that the meetings had something of a carnival atmosphere.

The announcement of the elections also raised the political temperature again and there were regular political meetings in the Fort Jameson African township. The organisers, of course, had to obtain a licence to hold these meetings, which our Messengers attended, both to make sure there was no trouble and to make a note of the substance of the speeches. As the date for the elections grew nearer, they reported that the speeches were becoming increasingly inflammatory and as the District Officers were in the front line, trying to keep electioneering within civilised bounds, we were often the subject of the speeches. Even I, with my area some distance away from the *boma*, received my fair share of the invective, although not as much, of course, as my senior colleagues with their areas near or including the township. The mild-mannered District Commissioner was, most unfairly, their favourite target. I have copied a letter, which the new Chairman saw fit to send me, which is fairly typical of the kind of literature which was circulating. It was easy to detect that the Provincial Commissioner was becoming increasingly frustrated and would dearly have loved to deal with the situation in a far more robust fashion than the political realities made sensible.

Perhaps as an escape from this he would from time to time make an excuse to do a day trip to the Valley with me. I had mixed feelings about these visitations. The Kunda were delighted to see the Provincial Commissioner and he obviously revelled in their old-fashioned courtesy, which, despite the troubles, by and large continued, certainly amongst

*Registering to vote – signing by thumbprint.*

the older generation. The trouble was that the Provincial Commissioner always insisted that we travel down in his official car, which was an enormous American beast which was the standard issue vehicle for Provincial Commissioners and above. They were chosen, I suppose, because they were large and impressive, particularly with a Union Jack pennant flying at the front, and they rode the corrugations well. The Provincial Commissioner was, of course, issued with a highly competent driver but on these trips usually elected to drive himself which, with his one arm and his penchant for driving extremely fast in the middle of the road, was a testing experience for his passengers. The experience was enlivened by the running commentary that he maintained and the fact that he always drove with the window open so that he could the better shout at other road users who, for one reason or another, had incurred his displeasure. The other disadvantage of the open window was that the rush of air tended to scatter the contents of his pipe, which was a permanent fixture between his lips. This led to his occasionally having to beat his breast, to extinguish the promising fires which, from time to time, took hold in his bush shirt. How he succeeded in doing this with his one arm and without losing control of the vehicle was as much a mystery as how he succeeded in changing gear (it was fortunately a gear shift on the steering wheel stalk) whilst at the same time filling his pipe. As I purported at the time to smoke a pipe myself, I was, if I was quick, able to get him to allow me at least to fill his pipe for him.

It was therefore no surprise that, when the time came for the new Paramount Chief to be installed, he insisted on joining the District Commissioner and other dignitaries from the *boma* at the ceremony. I took no part in organising the affair, but I was touched to find that the boys from Masumba in their uniforms had been brought along as a kind of youth corps to act as a guard of honour to the new Paramount Chief. I was less impressed when the Chief's party, including the party from the *boma* led by the Provincial Commissioner, suddenly found itself sur-rounded by a crowd of heavily decorated UNIP supporters, who obviously intended to take over the event. The party of Messengers and *kapassus*, which I had arranged to be present, moved quickly to prevent this and the Provincial Commissioner, like an old war horse, led the *boma* contingent in support, cuffing any opposition heads that came within reach. The Coronation accordingly started with an impressive little battle which the Government party just won. I have little recollection of what followed, save that I remember that the Provincial Commissioner, who had obviously enjoyed the fracas, made a stirring speech on behalf of the

Government. And Chief Jumbe felt it an appropriate moment to make a speech telling everyone that his clan and not the Nsefu clan should by rights provide the Paramount Chief. The new Paramount Chief was not called upon to make a speech and sat throughout with an expression of pop-eyed incomprehension surrounded by the Masumba boys and some very pretty young girls who had, we presumed, been recently recruited to his family. On the whole, however, the performance was hailed as a great success.

After this excitement life went back to normal. I continued to travel around, harassing my poor Kunda into the paths of righteousness. I used to spend hours in the Land-Rover, with my left arm hooked over the side through the open window, watching the Kunda world go by. By this time I had been in the Valley some eighteen months, and had spent considerably more time out on tour than I had in my office in the *boma*. As a result I had seen and been seen by a considerable proportion of my twenty-four thousand constituents so that as I drove around, very often with my mind on other things, I was subconsciously noting the faces we passed on the road. I began to notice if a face was out of place and would call a halt to enquire what he or she was doing or where they were going. It was amazing the picture that I began to build up of the life of the area.

Chief Malama, of course, got fairly regular visits, following the premature declaration of independence in his area, which also allowed me to call in at Masumba, where things continued to go well, and also at Chilongozi to see my game ranger friend. Chilongozi was a lovely reserve with the distinction of being the only reserve which could boast of having giraffe. It was also well-known for its lion. I always made a point of having a case of Castle lager with me when I visited. It was during my second dry season that at Chilongozi I had one of my narrowest escapes. We had had some excitement when the Gaboon viper, a beautiful, but to me unattractive, reptile that my game ranger friend (whose name alas I have completely forgotten) kept in a large box in his bedroom. He had taken the wire-mesh cover off the box to demonstrate to me how he kept his wallet in the box where it was perfectly safe. I had no reason to disagree with him, particularly when something diverted his attention and the snake, an adult only three-foot or so long but very thick and with a large flat head, slid unhurriedly out of the box and under his bed. Phiri had bravely come with me to see the snake and turned grey. I imagine that I, with a head start in the colour stakes, was even paler. My friend made no difficulty about rounding up the beast and returning it to its box but, perhaps as a result, the lager slipped down even better than usual so that we sat up until late swapping stories. He told me how a day before, he had seen a family of lion close to the track and had stopped to get a better look at them. For the same purpose he had walked a few paces into the bush where he climbed up a conveniently situated white ant mound. He stood on this for some time but could see nothing of the lion. It was not until he looked down, preparing to dismount from his vantage point, that he saw he had been about to put his foot on the head of one of several lionesses dozing in the shade of the mound. He must have nearly brushed past them without noticing, so good was their camouflage. His state of mind was not improved when he remembered that he had left his rifle in the Land-Rover. He had no alternative but to remain as still and as silent as possible until it pleased the lions to move off.

This tale prompted me to admit that I had never seen lion in the Valley and, of course, he volunteered that if I did not mind getting up early he would be happy to fill this gap in my education and take me to see a lioness and two cubs that had a lair in a dry river-bed close to the camp. So it was that a few hours later, just as it was beginning to get light, I found myself bouncing around in his Land-Rover and feeling rather hungover on my way to see the lions. Very soon he stopped and gestured to me to be quiet as he led the way a few yards to where, in the wet season, there would obviously be a considerable river. As we tiptoed up to the bank I could see, in the half-light, that there was a drop of about ten feet down to the dried bed of the river. The river, or at present the bed of the river, was some twenty-five yards wide and we were standing on the apex of a long bend in the course of the river. On our right, in which direction my ranger friend turned, the bank appeared to have collapsed under the weight of a tree which had fallen down the bank, taking the topsoil with it, and the whole tumble seemed to be covered with creeper of some kind. We stood for some time straining our eyes, as the light improved, towards the fallen tree where my friend had previously seen the lion. Nothing stirred. Eventually my friend suggested we clamber down into the river-bed itself. We slipped and jumped down on to the gravelly white sand which composed the river-bed and which was beginning to gleam in the rising sun. I was pleased to see that on this occasion my friend had prudently brought his rifle with him. It was not easy to move in the thick sand but we had advanced some yards away from the bank, when he stopped and whispered that he could see several lion half hidden by the creeper. I strained my eyes but could not see what was obvious to him. He was used to picking out the camouflaged shape of a lion and I was not. After a few minutes of frustration he whispered and gestured for me to pass in front of him but to keep low so as not to obscure his view of the lions. I accordingly crouched down and edged my way past him. Several things then happened at once. One adult lion leading two or maybe three cubs came out of the vegetation moving away from us round the corner and a second animal, a lioness, came bounding across the white sand towards us. I dropped on one knee, not as it happened in supplication, although from the undisguised look of evil intent on the face of the lioness this would have been prudent, but to give a clear field of fire to my friend the ranger who had, I saw out of the corner of my eye, thrown his rifle up to his shoulder and I heard him pump a shell into the breach. As soon as it became clear that the lioness meant business and had no intention of stopping, he fired. In the confined space of the river-bed the sound of the shot was very loud. The lioness, although she gave no sign of being shot, stopped and crouched low on the sand contemplating us with an expression of marked dislike. I noticed that she had a ruff, which was erect and framed her face and that her tail kept flicking in what I considered to be an ominous fashion. I also noticed that my ranger friend, whom I had last seen striking a rather heroic stance coolly aiming his rifle at the lioness, was now, for some unexplained reason, lying on his side behind me, apparently wrestling with his rifle. I was left with no alternative but to remain on one knee contemplating what was obviously a very angry lioness no more than ten yards away. I can honestly say that I did not feel frightened. I felt as though I was outside myself and watching, in a rather dispassionate way, to see what was going to happen next. What actually happened was that the lioness with one last snarl turned and having, I suppose, secured the cubs' retreat, loped off to rejoin them. My friend got back on to his feet. I thought he looked rather pale under his tan. No doubt I did also. Rather shakily I enquired how he could have been so sure that the lioness would stop when he shot over her head and why he had decided to lie down. He had not, he assured me, intended to shoot over the lioness's head. He had intended to hit her between the eyes but he had forgotten that his rifle was zeroed for a hundred and fifty yards and had not made any adjustment for the much closer range, so that his shot had gone over her head, albeit close enough, no doubt when taken with the noise of the shot, to make the lioness stop. And his lying on the sand? Oh, that was caused by his having lost his footing in the deep sand, and he was wrestling with his rifle because the next bullet that he was trying to load, to take a second shot, was defective and he could not get it into the breach. I asked for and was given the defective bullet as a memento.

As the year progressed the political activity increased and there was some ugly violence not, for a change, aimed in my direction but by one political party against the other. UNIP was very much in the ascendancy in the Valley, particularly amongst the younger generation, but there were enough of the older generation who preferred Mr Nkumbula and his ANC to cause trouble. The youth had a nasty habit of burning down the huts of known ANC supporters which, not surprisingly, irritated their elders and betters to the extent that they pulled their axes and spears out of what remained of their thatch and went on the warpath in earnest. I took to touring the troubled villages giving a graphic account (drawn happily entirely from my imagination) of the more gory details of a hanging, which in Northern Rhodesia at the time remained the penalty for murder. Most of the trouble at the time seemed to be in Chief Jumbe's area and I was pleased that the force of new *kapassus* was based there, near the Kunda Native Authority headquarters and that thirty-six of the reputedly most aggressive of the youths were out of circulation at Masumba.

It was at Jumbe that I had my last personal clash with UNIP. I had been visiting the Kunda headquarters building at Jumbe when word came in that there was trouble at the Indian stores (about a mile away). The first of the rains was imminent. I called for my driver who happened to be Chicomeni Banda and headed for the stores. For some reason James was not with me. I forget what the trouble was but I do remember that there was a crowd and that, although I needed to arrest the ringleader, the crowd was of such a size that when I invited the miscreant to 'come along with me' I hesitated actually to lay hands on him, which the crowd made quite clear they would be unhappy for me to do. As we stood discussing the matter the heavens opened and the rain, which had been threatening, descended in torrents in seconds drenching myself, Chicomeni and our potential prisoner. The crowd wisely retreated to the raised sidewalk under the shelter of the projecting roofs of the stores. I invited my prisoner to get into the Land-Rover. He refused. Chicomeni stood expectantly beside him, waiting for the order to assist him into the Land-Rover, with the rain pouring in a steady stream from the brim of his blue bush hat which, like his blue uniform, had turned black in the rain. I did not want to lose face by abandoning the man whom I had determined to arrest, but at the same time I did not want to escalate the incident by attempting to arrest the man in front of his home crowd, as it were, and so I compromised and suggested that we should walk together to the Kunda headquarters building. To my relief the man agreed and I accordingly directed Chicomeni to get back into the Land-Rover and to drive slowly on ahead of us. My prisoner and I walked along in the lashing rain behind the Land-Rover in the direction of the headquarters. The crowd, having made its point, sensibly decided to remain in the dry. We walked on for perhaps two hundred yards until we were just about out of sight of the stores, whereupon the Land-Rover came to an abrupt halt in front of us, and Chicomeni got out and unhurriedly, and entirely without orders, plodded through the rain to the rear of the Land-Rover where, without even a glance at me, he picked up the prisoner by his belt and the scruff of his neck. I have already described Chicomeni's physique and need not do so again; suffice it to say that he raised the man (who was a tall, rangy individual) above his head and literally threw him into the back of the Land-Rover. He then stomped back to the front of the vehicle and, without further comment, proceeded to drive me via the headquarters back to the *boma*, where we handed the man over to the Police to prosecute.

In fact the rains rather caught me out that year. The Masumba scheme was due to end as soon as the rains started, but I had allowed the time to pass without making the necessary arrangements for the passing-out parade, and now the rains had started with unexpected vigour. I then received word that there had been trouble in Mnkanya's area near Masumba. I had no alternative but to head for the Valley, praying that the river at Jumbe did not rise too high for me to get through. As soon as I got to Jumbe I headed straight for the ford over which the main road passed on its way to the game parks and Masumba. I groaned as I saw the foaming torrent that had replaced the usual trickle of water which barely topped the concrete apron which was laid across the sandy bed of the river to prevent vehicles bogging in the deep sand. I was used to seeing the river in flood and to joining the crowd that usually formed on these occasions to watch which vehicles attempted the crossing, and with what success, and which decided that discretion was the better part of valour and turned away to wait for the river to fall. I myself had had some close shaves in the Land-Rover, to the extent of having the passengers, including myself, leap out when the engine flooded. I had seen the wreck of the heavily loaded lorry which had been swept away, having wrongly relied on its weight to keep it on the ford, and had marvelled at the fury of the flood that had succeeded in doing so. Now at last I could see for myself just what a real flood looked like. This was no common-or-garden little flood which flooded engines and made Land-Rovers wobble. This was a proper serious flood, which tore past, twenty-foot deep, threatening to overflow the steep banks between which it sped with an ominous hissing. On the other side of the river, some thirty yards away, was the Kunda Native Authority lorry and what looked like faces from the Masumba team. They obviously wanted to tell us something but try as we might we could not hear them. I stood and pondered for some time. I did not like the look of the water. There was no question of James trying to swim it, and although I did not formally ask them, it was clear from their expressions that the other younger Messengers were not very keen either. In the event I decided I should try. I accordingly walked at least a hundred yards up river before wading in. I say wading but, in reality, no sooner had I entered the water than I was swept away. I had kept my clothes on but the water was quite warm and all I had to do was to swim as hard as I could across the stream, with the result that I travelled at an angle that, incredibly quickly, took me in view of the crowd at the crossing and the reception committee waiting for me on the other side. It was just as well that I had gone as far upstream as I had because, despite my best endeavours, I only just got within reach of the hands that stretched out to catch me at the far side, before being swept on. Both the Police Inspector and a Messenger and a *kapassu* were waiting for me and insisted on saluting me as the water ran off me. They had been waiting for twenty-four hours, they told me. They knew I would come as soon as the rains started, although how they knew I would try to come that very day, when I myself had only decided that morning to do so, I do not know. In any event, they went on brightly, the boys were all ready for my inspection and what was I proposing to do with their prisoners who were getting hungry. 'What prisoners?' I enquired. It emerged that a gang of UNIP youths had been terrorising Chief Mnkanya's area (no doubt assuming that no one could get at them because of the floods) and the Chief had sent to Masumba for assistance. The Police Inspector had not hesitated to respond to the call and, with the approval of my VSO, had recruited the boys on the course (overlooking their previous records) to assist, pointing out that, as they had been eating food provided by the Government for the past six months, the least they could do was to lend the Government a hand in its hour of need. The boys had, it seemed, enthusiastically agreed and so the Kunda lorry, which had fortuitously been in the area, had been commandeered and the boys and all available Messengers and *kapassus* loaded into it and driven to the rescue. The UNIP gang, confronted with what must have appeared overwhelming force, had immediately capitulated and been arrested with due formality by the enterprising Inspector and taken back to Masumba where (there were a dozen or so of them) they were busy eating the camp out of food while they waited for me to provide transport back to the *boma*.

The first thing, as everyone insisted, was to hold a closing ceremony and to hand out the certificates in thatching, carpentry and bricklaying that the Kunda headquarters had supplied and to congratulate the boys, and indeed the staff, on what had been a most successful venture. I confess to having little recollection of the formalities, which is not surprising, as I was trying to work out how to convey a dozen or so prisoners over a flooded river and on to the *boma*. Accordingly as soon as the boys had left in groups, singing on their way back to their villages, the Kunda lorry was loaded up with the staff, and the prisoners and myself, and driven back to the river. There the staff and the prisoners were left to fend for themselves as best they could, while I recrossed the river in the same fashion as I had crossed it earlier in the day, and drove back to the *boma* to get transport for the prisoners from Jumbe and, more pertinently, some means of transporting them across the flood which showed no sign of abating.

There was nothing to be done that night but the next day I persuaded the District Commissioner to lend me the *boma* lorry and on it I loaded a number of empty forty-four gallon oil drums, a rudimentary kind of metal boat that I commandeered from a road gang, some planks and a great deal of rope of various sizes and, most important, a block and tackle which I succeeded in borrowing from PWD. I also suggested that they might like to lend me someone who was used to building rafts to ferry prisoners across flooded rivers, but they replied, most politely that although, of course, they had any number of people who had plenty of experience in that kind of thing, unfortunately none of them was immediately available or indeed would be available for the foreseeable future. It was accordingly left to me and a posse of Messengers to head back to Jumbe to organise the evacuation. The river had indeed dropped a little, but nothing like sufficiently to allow the lorry to cross. We accordingly set to, to build a crude raft out of the oil drums lashed on to some of the planks. Of course, the raft when built and, in the first instance, the boat, would have to be attached to a rope, both to avoid them being washed away and to give them a means of propulsion. The first step was to get the rope over the river and so once again I took to the water with a rope around my waist, despite the fact that the crowd, rather tactlessly I thought, had insisted that I should inspect the corpse of a man who had been drowned the previous day trying to cross the river in the same place as I was about to try to cross.

Anyway, I successfully crossed the river and the boat was duly attached and with many willing hands on the rope it was pulled across the river with me on it. The prisoners were interested spectators of this activity and indeed had pulled on the rope with enthusiasm but when it was suggested to them that they should allow themselves to be transported on the boat or, when it was completed, the raft, they politely but firmly declined the privilege. In vain did I point out that I had just crossed the river on the boat. That was quite different, they said. You are an *Msungu* (European) and can swim. Nothing that I or the Inspector could say would move them and I was in despair what to do when it occurred to me to crave the assistance of my wife, who had, fortuitously and unusually, obtained leave to come with me for the trip. I recrossed the river and explained the difficulty and suggested that, if she were prepared to cross the river on the raft, the prisoners might be shamed into doing so. She was a trifle dubious, rightly so, as she was not a strong swimmer, but in the event allowed herself to be a guinea pig and crossed and recrossed the river. Following her example, the prisoners and the Masumba staff were safely pulled across the river and loaded onto the lorry and, in due course, transported to Fort Jameson Police Station. I made a point of going a few minutes ahead of the lorry to prepare the Police for a number of unexpected malefactors and giving credit for their capture to one of their own Inspectors. My news caused a considerable stir, and the Station Commander was called, who wanted to know which of his African Inspectors had succeeded in arresting a dozen or so malcontents, apparently single-handed. When I gave him the name of the Inspector and explained how he had been assisting with a youth training scheme in the Valley for the past few months, for which I was, I assured him, extremely grateful, he turned very red and demanded to know by what authority I had, without his permission or even knowledge, 'borrowed' one of his more senior officers and installed him on his own in the Valley. Happily he was an Irishman and soon saw the funny side of the situation – his precious Inspector, whom he thought he had lost, being stolen by a very junior officer, only to reappear with a crew of prisoners. Fortunately, he did not take the matter any further.

The elections took place in January 1964 during the rains. No doubt there was a good reason for this but it was difficult to think of one. I was not an election official but I was involved in helping to organise the

*A reluctant guinea pig.*

mechanics of the election in the Valley and in keeping law and order during the process. I based myself at my old camp under the baobab trees at Masumba. I installed one of the several Returning Officers who were required for the Valley in Jumbe. Another Returning Officer I took with me to Masumba from where he was to set off early the next morning on a bicycle to the local school, which was to serve as the polling station. He took with him his crew of assistants, similarly mounted, and carrying all that they required. This was more of a struggle than it would appear as the equipment included sacking screens as well as the usual tin ballot boxes. Precariously loaded with their screens, they looked like some strange sailing craft as they set off through the mud. It was quite an adventure for some of the Returning Officers. It should be understood that in addition to the expatriate administrative and professional officers, there were middle-ranking officers, both European and African, some expatriate and some recruited locally, whose employment kept them permanently in an office in provincial centres, so that even in a little place like Fort Jameson, they lived a typically suburban life, which revolved around the tennis courts, the golf course and the club. For officers such as these, a trip into the Valley, even for one night, was a great adventure. They had no idea what it was like in even the limited 'bush' that they were to penetrate and which I am sure they were convinced was heavily populated with lions and tigers.

In the event the elections went off quietly, certainly in the Valley, and UNIP, as expected, swept in with a huge majority. The African majority government was not due to take over until October, when there were to be vast Independence celebrations. Until that date everything was to continue as before. The only exception to this was that a new office of Junior Minister was introduced to represent the government in each province and in due course to replace the Provincial Commissioners. As part of the system of 'shadowing', which had been in existence for some time in the ministry headquarters in Lusaka, these Junior Ministers were appointed in advance of Independence. Our local incumbent invited himself out with the District Officers to get to know the area for which he would shortly be politically responsible. That included a trip to the Valley to meet the Chiefs and Councillors. I did not travel with him but met him down in the Valley and sat beside him at a meeting which was called in his honour. I forget the Minister's name but he was obviously intelligent and spoke excellent English and was dressed sensibly in bush shirt, shorts and long socks – the perfect Provincial Commissioner, in fact.

I confess to some apprehension as the meeting started. I had after all been vigorous in my pursuit of the Minister's political colleagues in the Valley if they had stepped out of line. Sure enough, as soon as the Minister had finished his opening speech, welcoming the brave new world that was about to dawn, various members of the audience, none of whom I recognised and none of them the senior officers of UNIP, whom I would have expected to complain, leaped to their feet to demand that I be reprimanded for my harassment of the faithful. These demands were accompanied by highly-coloured and largely imaginary examples of my infliction of gross injustices on the law-abiding people of the Kunda Valley. Many of their complaints were to do with my insistence that the Councillors should not allow the Kunda Native Authority lorry, that overworked beast of burden, to be used for political purposes, by which they meant transporting UNIP officers and gangs of their young supporters around the Valley.

Any worries I might have had that the Minister might have been tempted to acquire easy political kudos by reprimanding me were quickly dispelled. He brushed aside the complaints (this had all been in the past and was of no interest) and he assured his chastened audience that the new African government was going to be at least as strict about the lorry as was the present administration. I am not sure that this intention was put into practice, as highly-coloured tales circulated that in Lusaka a dozen of the Chevrolets that were issued to the new Ministers were, within hours of being issued, written off in accidents by their over-enthusiastic owners or their UNIP drivers out of office hours. Despite this conciliatory attitude on the part of the new regime, the Provincial Commissioner retired. Whether he jumped or whether he was pushed, I do not know. We attended the dinner party he gave at the Provincial Commissioner's residence to mark the occasion, which was a sad affair.

I had always been reassured, when out on tour sometimes in fairly hairy circumstances, that at least my wife was in no danger at home and that any of my parishioners who wanted to take revenge for anything I might have done to offend them would be prevented from doing so by the sensible arrangement that, when an officer was away on tour, a Messenger was sent to mount guard on his house. In fact, I noticed that on the occasions that my wife could get away on tour with me the minor, and sometimes major, demonstrations that often marked my progress appeared to be suspended, I suspect out of courtesy to her, the argument being, I suppose, that if I could demonstrate my trust in their good manners to bring my wife with me, they would not want to breach that trust. Perhaps that was pure imagination but the fact remains that never in all the times that my wife visited the Valley was she ever involved in, nor even saw, any sign of trouble. In any event it happened that one night when I was away on tour there was a break-in at our house. Due to a mix-up, the normal Messenger guard had not been posted. My wife had woken when the dog, still not much more than a puppy, who was sharing her bed, moved and she was aware that there was someone in the room. She bravely called out and the man fled, pursued by the now very wide-awake dog. Happily the man got away through the kitchen door, which he had left open as a line of retreat. When she got back to her bedroom, my wife found the mark of a dirty hand on her sheet just beside her pillow, presumably where the man had leant when he bent down to look for her handbag. Nothing was taken and no harm done, but it was an extremely unpleasant experience for my wife. Word of the burglary was brought to me in the valley. I was furious and drove immediately back to the *boma*, where I marched in to see the District Commissioner whom I upbraided, no doubt most unfairly bearing in mind his other worries, for not ensuring that the Messenger had been posted. After that, however, we tended to be less trusting, a sentiment which was obviously shared by our servants. We were out late one night, I cannot remember why, but this, like most of our movements, was known to our servants. When we got back in the early hours we saw, in the lights of the motor car, a figure lurking round the side of the house. As we pulled up outside the house Phiri appeared, smiling broadly and with his knobkerrie under his arm. There had been some trouble in the African township where he lived and on his own initiative, and knowing that we were going to be out late, he decided to mount guard.

I had hitherto escaped any kind of illness but in the early part of what was to be my final year in the Valley I fell ill. My temperature was very high and the doctor who was called diagnosed malaria and ordered me off to hospital. As malaria was so rife, the medical profession diagnosed everything as malaria. Certainly I was very ill for a few days and could do nothing but lie in bed and alternately sweat and freeze. The European hospital was a pleasant enough place, set high up on the hills that surrounded Fort Jameson, with wide verandas and passages to keep the building cool. The passages were, like most floors, painted red and polished each day. As soon as word reached James that I was ill, he got permission from the Senior Messenger and, abandoning his post outside my office, set off on his bicycle to visit me and see how I was doing. He visited each day and, although I was not up to talking or indeed doing anything very much, I was conscious of his visits. The first indication of his arrival was some heavy stamping from a long way away, as James in his service-issue boots marched, and I mean marched, from the entrance hall along the corridors towards the ward which I shared with two or three other men. The footsteps got closer and eventually halted outside the ward, where James apparently paused to gather his thoughts. After a moment or two James would enter the room, obviously trying to march silently but undoubtedly still marching. He would come to a halt at the foot of my bed, as I could see through my heavy eyelids, and then salute my prone figure. After a further pause he would then whisper, compassionately 'Velly solly, velly solly'. Another pause and then he would salute again, turn smartly about and I would then hear his departing footsteps echoing down the corridors as he returned to duty at the *boma*.

I had barely recovered from malaria or, as I strongly suspected, a bad bout of flu, when a message came for me over the police radio that my father had had to have another urgent operation and, although he had come through it all right, he was still critically ill and I should drop everything and get down to Lusaka as soon as I could. If we left pretty well at once and travelled all night, we could be at his bedside by early the next morning. Although much better, I was still in hospital and it was doubtful whether I could drive even half the way with my wife driving the other half, which, on the corrugations, was in itself problematic, and so I borrowed a Messenger driver to help drive our car and generally to provide support, and set out.

It is some 350 miles along the Great East Road between Fort Jameson and Lusaka. In the early 1960s it was compacted gravel all the way, except for a few miles between Fort Jameson and the airport, which was on the Lusaka road, and for a few miles outside Lusaka. In the dry season vehicles kicked up an enormous plume of dust so that trying to overtake a lorry, often with a trailer, was a hazardous enterprise to say the least. It was most unlikely that the lorry driver would have seen a vehicle in his mirror trying to overtake, partly because his attention would be concentrated on avoiding the enormous potholes with which the road was pockmarked, and partly because the overtaking vehicle would be obscured by the dust until it got virtually alongside the driver. The best plan was to wait well back from the lorry, until a hill or a bend gave a view of the road a mile or so ahead, and then accelerate like mad through the sand that billowed up for a hundred yards or so behind the lorry, trying to ignore the damage that the unseen potholes were doing to the chassis, to get in front of it before something appeared in the road that you had scouted. If there were no hills or bends then you either possessed your soul in patience and trundled along behind the lorry or you took your life in your hands and battled through the dust plume until you got to the back of the lorry, when you pulled out and overtook, praying hard that an enormous lorry would not suddenly appear through the dust travelling fast in the opposite direction. In either event it was an extremely stressful exercise and not to be undertaken by the faint-hearted.

In the event, and by changing drivers, we did the ten-hour journey in record time, despite a short delay occasioned by one of the huge lorries having lost its way on one of the bends in the road, where it wound tortuously through some hills, and ended up completely blocking the road and with its nose in a stream- bed. Extremely fortunately, this contretemps happened in daylight and, even more fortuitously, the new Provincial Commissioner, on his way in his new Chevrolet to Fort Jameson to take over the Eastern Province, was also blocked. After some discussion we decided that although there was no possibility of getting the Chevrolet past, we might with some manhandling, get our VW through the bush and across the stream-bed and back on to the road. And so indeed it happened that, with the sterling assistance of the new Provincial Commissioner and his driver, we got through, promising to send help from the first village we came to.

We duly arrived early the next morning at Lusaka and went straight to the hospital to see my father. He was obviously a very ill man and the doctor confirmed that his cancer was terminal. The immediate problem was that his kidneys had stopped working and there was no knowing whether they would start up again. We made the decision to send for my brother to fly out, despite the cost, in the expectation that it would be lucky if my father survived long enough to see him. Despite the pessimistic prognosis, my father not only survived to see my brother but was so thrilled by his arrival (we had not told him that my brother was on his way) that miraculously his kidneys started working again. That at least was the explanation that we gave. Alternatively, and more prosaically, someone pointed out to my father, whose faculties remained unimpaired, that if he survived until, I think it must have been Independence Day on the 24 October, his pension would be considerably enhanced, and he was so determined to get the better of the government that he defied medical opinion. Whatever the cause, the fact is that he did survive and was sufficiently well to be flown home to Gloucestershire where he was nursed by my mother until the end. He died aged only fifty-three.

Back in Fort Jameson life went on pretty well as before. My mother-in-law visited again and again I got permission to take some local leave so as to be able to explore the country. The first place on our list was Lundazi, a district headquarters just over a hundred miles to the north of Fort Jimmy. Within its district boundaries it boasted game reserves on the Northern Luangwa and, to the north, on the border with Nyasaland, the Nyika plateau. Perhaps its main claim to fame, however, was the fact that there was situated near the *boma* wonderful 'Rumpelstilt-skin' Castle, complete with turrets, battlements, arrow slits and a dungeon. Prosaically it was known as the Castle Hotel. It had been built not many years before as a glorified rest house by an enterprising District Commissioner, Errol Button, to provide for the accommodation of the visitors who were beginning to come to Lundazi on their way to the Luangwa or the Nyika plateau. What inspired him to allow his imagination to run riot in order to build a fairy-tale castle, in place of the usual square utilitarian monstrosities which were the government norm, I do not know, but the result, all made out of local materials by local craftsmen, was, we were told, spectacular.

We decided in the first instance to do a day trip to spy out the land and then, if we liked it, to visit again and spend a day or two and visit the Nyika plateau. We talked our plans over with our friends, Bernard, who had just been transferred to Fort Jimmy to be the new District Officer Chewa, and Paddy, his wife. We decided to make a really early start, both to give us plenty of time to explore Lundazi and to be able to travel in the cool of the day. Soon after dawn Paddy telephoned to say that the District Commissioner was away and so Bernard was acting District Commissioner and had been called out in the early hours because there was serious trouble in Lundazi. She suggested I ought to drop in at the *boma* to make sure it was all right for us to visit Lundazi. While my wife and her mother dressed, I pulled on some clothes and drove down to the *boma*. Bernard was looking grave, as well he might. He had received word that the Lenshinas in the Eastern Province, working in concert with their brethren across the Luangwa, had gone on the warpath, sweeping through Lundazi, attacking and taking the police station and killing over a hundred people. He was trying to contact the District Commissioner in Lundazi but there was no reply from the *boma* and either the District Commissioner and his District Officer were out on tour or he feared they had been killed in their beds. To make matters worse the interim Provincial Commissioner, whom I had met on the road to Lusaka, had gone on leave and although his replacement was on his way he had not yet arrived. Someone from the Provincial Administration needed urgently to go up to Lundazi and find out what had happened to the District Commissioner and, if he could not be found, hold the fort until the District Commissioner could be found or replaced. 'He would like to go but with both the District Commissioner and Provincial Commissioner away . . .' The Messengers had already been summoned to report to the *boma*. Ignoring James's outraged expression I chose, with the assistance of the Senior Messenger, six ex-Askari Messengers and Chicomeni as my driver, all of whom I sent off to collect their bedding rolls and then to report back to the *boma* to be issued with rifles and ammunition. Half an hour later, after I made a very brief stop at home to explain the situation and to collect the minimum of clothes, the Land-Rover, with the Messengers looking very warlike with their rifles between their knees, was at the door to collect me.

Although I had been too much taken up with the Kunda Valley to pay attention to it, the Lenshinas, or more accurately members of the Lumpa Church, founded by Alice Lenshina in the Chinsali District of the Northern Province, had often been in trouble and in the news as a result of problems with both the authorities and UNIP, Chinsali being a hotbed of Nationalist political activity. Alice Lenshina was reputed to look like, and was, a typical village woman until she had a vision, telling her to preach against witchcraft, which by all accounts was rife in Chinsali District. Apparently she began her mission within one of the Evangelical Christian Church Missions in the district but soon fell out with them and set up her own church, a strange blend of Evangelical Christianity and African tradition and superstition. There was certainly no doubt as to the loyalty she inspired in her followers, as demonstrated by the 'Cathedral' that was built for her in her home village. There had been conflict, some years previously, with the local Chiefs, who resented the challenge she represented to their authority, and subsequently with the District Commissioner, who was forced to call in the Police Mobile Unit. Eventually, and with no little difficulty, some of the leaders were arrested and the disturbance was quelled but not until there had been some loss of life, including at least one European officer. More recently there had been trouble between UNIP and the Church and again the Mobile Unit had been called in and again the Lenshinas had reacted violently, succeeding in chasing off the Unit on several occasions and inflicting casualties on them. The Lenshinas were eventually defeated, with considerable loss, but not until the Army had been called in.

The Lumpa Church had for some time operated in the Lundazi district of the Eastern province and this attack was obviously connected with what had been happening to their brethren in Chinsali.

# CHAPTER 6

# Lundazi

WE COVERED THE MILES at breakneck speed and arrived in Lundazi late in the morning. I recall it as a pleasant little town with plenty of mature trees. The entire population seemed to be gathered in a large grassy area in the middle of the town. I must have been to the *boma* and the Police Station, the latter of which had been sacked, but I confess to having no recollection of what I found. What I do recall is the panic of the crowd. I had the difficulty that the people in Lundazi were a different tribe to those in the Fort Jimmy area and so I could not communicate with them except through an interpreter. As we drove onto the grassy area the crowd which had gathered there surged around us and a schoolmaster attached himself to me as an unofficial interpreter. I and the Messengers tried to discover from the people exactly what had happened. There was no difficulty in finding people bursting to tell their tale, but they were badly rattled and it was difficult to extract a coherent story. The best we could piece together was that several hundred Lenshinas had swept through the township that night, stabbing and hacking to death anyone they found. It was thought that both the District Commissioner and his District Officer were out on tour and had therefore escaped the slaughter. It subsequently emerged that nearly two hundred people of various ages and sexes had been killed and another fifty or sixty had been wounded. No Europeans, they thought, had been harmed, although they were not sure about the European couple who ran the Lundazi Castle Hotel. Rumours constantly swept the crowd which numbered, I guess, the best part of a thousand. Suddenly from one side of the ground or the other the cry would go up, 'They are coming!' and immediately the crowd would surge across the ground away from the expected point of attack. Heart thumping I loaded the Messengers, who had got out to talk to the crowd, and drove towards the area from which it was rumoured the attack was coming. For the first time or two that this happened, when I got to the end of the grassed area nearest to where the attack was said to be imminent, I ordered the Messengers (who had already at my order loaded their rifles) to spread out and take up firing positions. After the third or fourth false alarm we simply drove the Land-Rover across to the

threatened area with me sitting on the bonnet of the vehicle calling out
to the crowd not to panic and reassuring them, with easy mendacity, that
we would protect them.

This went on for some hours during which period I was the nearest
thing that the government had to a presence on the ground. The first
person to relieve me was, I believe, the District Commissioner from Fort
Jameson with another load of Messengers and then the advance guard of
the Northern Rhodesia Regiment arrived by air onto the little grass strip
just outside the *boma*. After that everyone started to appear. The first
demand of the army was for transport, they having arrived by air, and
they were not very particular how they acquired it. As soon as I could I
went to visit the hotel. The couple who ran the hotel under some kind
of arrangement with the government had had a very lucky escape. They
had heard the Lenshinas prowling, like the hosts of Midian, around the
hotel, and had hidden themselves in case they got in. They were a strange
couple, she large and English and he small, bearded and French. He was
a swimming instructor by trade. I forget by what strange circumstance
they had ended up running a fantasy castle hotel in the middle of Africa.
I have a recollection that she had been something of a heroine, in having
insisted on going out early in the morning to discover what had
happened, and had alerted the authorities to the massacre. In any event
by the time I visited them they were open for business and ready to
welcome the relieving forces that were starting to arrive and required
accommodation. It was fortunate that, despite being so junior, I got a
room as a result of being an early arrival.

To complicate matters the interim Provincial Commissioner had left
the province and, although his successor was on his way, there was no
one, in the absence of the Lundazi District Commissioner, to take
command of a most difficult situation, except our own District
Commissioner from Fort Jimmy as acting Provincial Commissioner. His
first priority, and that of the commanding officer of the Northern
Rhodesia Regiment, when he arrived with the advance guard, after
satisfying himself that the town was secure, was to ensure that there was
no further attack by the Lenshinas, who had withdrawn to their fortified
village of Chipoma, a few miles outside Lundazi, beyond the airport. As
the troops flew in, it was therefore ordered that there was to be an attack
made on Chipoma village as soon as it could be mounted the next day.
One of the Lundazi District Officers reappeared, either during the night
or early the next day, and was appointed to accompany the Colonel as
the representative of the civil power in the advance on the village.

Incredibly, by the time the advance on the village was mounted late the next morning some seven or eight representatives of the world's press had arrived and were demanding to have a ringside seat for the action. They were accommodated for this purpose in a long-wheel, covered-in Land-Rover. I was ordered to take charge of the gentlemen of the press and to be sure, on pain of death, to keep them out of the Colonel's way at the rear of the convoy, which formed in preparation for the advance on Chipoma. Ominously, one of the aircraft which had been flying in the troops had crashed, and although no one had been injured, it had caught fire and a pall of oily black smoke billowed over us as we passed by the end of the runway. We did not yet know the truth of the matter until later and, as we drove through the smoke, we did not know the reason for the crash and whether it might have been caused by the Lenshinas or whether or not there had been any loss of life. I and my eight Messengers brought up the rear of the long convoy with the press Land-Rover immediately in front of us.

Eventually the convoy halted, presumably, (because I was too far back to see anything) to offload the troops. When eventually the press and I got to the head of the queue, I found that the lorries which had been carrying the troops had been left unattended in a clearing in the bush. With the thought that the burning aircraft might have had something to do with the Lenshinas operating in our rear and that they might do the same kind of thing to the lorries, I took it upon myself to leave my Messengers with their rifles to guard the lorries, while I, with one Messenger and Chicomeni as Messenger/driver, went on with the press corps, who were already demanding to move forward to see the action. I left my Messengers calmly loading their rifles and, under the direction of the Senior Messenger, spreading out in defensive positions around the lorries.

I took care to put my Land-Rover in front of the press corps vehicle and drove cautiously on to the crest of a gentle slope leading down to the village of Chipoma where, being very conscious of my orders to keep well to the rear and keep the press safe and out of the way of the Colonel, I halted. Although the slope down to the village was clear, being cultivated as gardens so that we had a clear view of all that was happening, the press were not content and demanded that they be allowed to move forward. I explained my orders, but one or two of them became belligerent and, after a fair amount of abuse, made as if to ignore my directions and walk on to catch up with the troops. I was worrying about my decision to leave the Messengers with the lorries and what would happen if I was right and the Lenshinas attacked us in the rear. They would, if in sufficient numbers, soon overrun my handful of Messengers with their rifles. With that worry on my mind I was not going to put up with the wretched pressmen agitating to go and make a nuisance of themselves amongst the troops. I accordingly seized the rifle from my remaining Messenger and, putting a bullet in the chamber, I warned them that I would put a bullet into the first of them that attempted to move past me. I must have looked fairly convincing because no further effort was made to go on past me. Instead they contented themselves with clambering up onto the top of their Land-Rover to get a better view.

The troops in open order were advancing slowly on the village with weapons at the ready. Chipoma was a large village, almost a small town. I would estimate it would have had a population of around a thousand. It was surrounded by some kind of stockade made of tree trunks and branches. There was clearly some kind of meeting going on in the village. There was a crowd and they were being harangued, presumably by one of their leaders. There was a great deal of shouting. The crowd was obviously being worked up for action. The recently returned District Officer, dressed in his white office uniform, to make him clearly visible, was walking among the leading troops calling out through a loud hailer for the villagers to come out quietly and unarmed to avoid the troops opening fire. This was very brave of him because there was a strong suspicion that the Lenshinas did have at least one firearm. No response was made to the District Officer's appeals. Instead the crowd erupted from the village and spread out with the obvious intention of surrounding the troops.

One of the arms of their advance was headed beyond and behind where the press and I were standing on top of our slope. The press were busy photographing this until there was an outraged yell from the top of the press Land-Rover and, with one accord and considerable alacrity, the press corps vacated their grandstand seats and instead went to earth under the Land-Rover. From there they demanded, with the same urgency as they had previously demanded to see more of the action, that I should protect them. Apparently one of the more belligerent of them had had a bullet go through a fold in his shirt. Although it had not actually touched him it had, not surprisingly, given him a nasty shock, causing him to yell and throw himself off the top of the Land-Rover, with such alacrity that he had actually overtaken in the air one of his colleagues who had jumped off the vehicle a few moments before him. Certainly the man had a hole in his shirt to confirm his story and give substance to the rumour that the Lenshinas had a firearm. However, no one else other than Lenshinas were shot, and no firearm was ever found. In any event it clearly made sense to move forward to be nearer the troops, who were beginning to open fire on the Lenshinas, many of them women who, brandishing a variety of weapons, charged at the soldiers. Despite the casualties and with ridiculous bravery they kept coming on. We heard later that the leaders had promised that bullets could not hurt them. Where we were, at the rear, the Lenshinas were pretty thin on the ground, but one old lady waving a stick kept coming and a young soldier shot her in the arm. A White Father, who had somehow managed to accompany the troops, went forward to help her and I went with him. As we tried to put some kind of dressing on the wound, to our horror, one of the gentlemen of the press tried to take it off so that he could get a better picture of the wound. I fussed and worried about my Messengers and tried to get permission to drive back to them, which was very properly refused, and in the event when I was reunited with them I found them to have been in no danger.

We eventually entered the village and the press had a field day taking pictures of the horrors. The White Father made the front pages of the papers, cuddling children whom he had rescued from the shambles in the village. So also did a doctor (not English) who gave interviews to the press while operating on the wounded. I helped load the bodies of the dead (there were eighty or so of them) onto flatbed lorries which were hidden under guard for the night. I was ordered to supervise their burial in a mass grave early the next morning.

It had been an extremely unpleasant experience. It was impossible not to feel that it should have been possible to have disarmed and arrested the Lenshinas without shooting so many of them. The fit young soldier who shot the old lady, for instance, could have taken the stick she was carrying off her with one muscular arm tied behind his back. Perhaps that was an isolated example. It is true that these were the self-same people, or at least some of them were, who had massacred some two hundred innocent people in their beds the night before. Certainly the Colonel, who gave the order to open fire, was entitled, and indeed under a duty, to carry out his orders with the least risk to his men. The Lenshinas had been given more than adequate warning to throw down their weapons (however impotent they might seem in comparison to the automatic rifles of the soldiers) and it could well be argued that it did not make sense to risk trying to disarm even a female Lenshina by hand, even at minimal risk, when the soldier could do so at no risk at all by using his rifle. The Colonel was also entitled to take into account that he had just come from the Northern Province where the Lenshinas had routed a unit of the Police Mobile Unit and that they were reputed to have at least one firearm available to them.

We expatriate officers could not, however, be unaffected by the knowledge that the Lenshinas had received a great deal of harassment from UNIP, the lower echelons of which had little sympathy with the claim of the Lenshinas that they had no interest in politics and regarded membership of UNIP as conflicting with loyalty to their church. It seemed too much of a coincidence not to attribute the present trouble to the realisation by the Lenshinas that, with the coming to power of a UNIP Government, they could in future expect little mercy, whatever the efforts of Kenneth Kaunda and the hierarchy of his party to reassure them to the contrary.

Among the representatives of all kinds of strange departments and organisations who, over the next few days discovered that they had something to contribute to the situation, appeared senior representatives of the African Government in waiting. Although at pains to assure the expatriate civil servants, who were dealing with the matter, that they had no intention of wanting to take over responsibility for the decisions that had to be taken, they left them in no doubt that they expected them to clear things up before they took over and were not concerned at how drastic any solution might be.

The next morning before dawn I set off with the Messengers to escort the lorries, carrying the bodies of the dead Lenshinas, into the outskirts of Lundazi where a grave had been prepared. As luck would have it, our way back lay past the airfield and, although it was only just light, I was horrified to see what was, from the cameras draped around him, obviously some kind of reporter just arrived, I guessed, on an early morning flight. The lorries piled high with corpses and dripping with blood would provide a shot no reporter could resist and I shuddered to think of the headlines the pictures would create and the odium that would fall on my shoulders for having allowed them to be taken. Sure enough I saw the man reach for his camera and then to my surprise and infinite relief, after a pause, put it back on his shoulder again without taking a picture. I made it my business to speak to him later and asked why he had not taken some shots. 'There are some things it is better not to photograph,' he explained with a shrug.

Under the direction of a local Messenger we turned off in the outskirts of the town down a track and into a wooded area well away, presumably,

from prying eyes and where a bulldozer had excavated a grave for the
bodies. It stood ready to fill the soil in on top of them. Some labourers
from the *boma* stood waiting ready to unload the lorries. I was just about
to give the order to start when I was horrified to see a small crowd of
people, led by another local Messenger (who had, presumably as a result
of his position, heard of the burial), advancing down the track. I called
out through an interpreter to know what they wanted. They replied to
the effect that they just wanted to see, and presumably gloat at, the bodies
being buried. Perhaps the Messenger had a relative who had been killed
by the Lenshinas. I did not care. Leaving aside the fact that it was
macabre to carry out an unpleasant task under the eyes of an audience,
my orders made clear I was to carry out the burial with as little publicity
as possible. I accordingly ordered the Messenger and his friends to go
away and emphasised this order, in case he did not understand my
Chinyanja, with an appropriate pantomime. He appeared not to hear me
and indeed he looked either as though he was drugged or in a state of
shock. He was an elderly little chap with a shotgun over his shoulder, an
understandable precaution in the circumstances. More to attract his
attention than anything else, I put up my hand and tapped on the back
of his head. I succeeded in attracting his attention all right. With one
fluid movement, and giving a cry of anger, he aimed a blow with the
butt of his shotgun at my head. I instinctively ducked and turned away,
and so avoided the full force of the blow, but it still caught me a glancing
blow on the back of my head. I was knocked dizzy for a moment, but
not too dizzy not to see him fire the shotgun at me from his hip at point
blank range. How he missed from that range I do not know, but miss he
did. I then watched unbelieving as he proceeded to put another shell into
his gun, presumably with the intention of having another shot at me. I
did not wait to find out but turned and ran, dodging as I went, returning
only when the Messengers, who had been apparently frozen in disbelief
that one of their number should have attempted to kill a District Officer
whom it was their duty to protect, came to life and seized the man and
took the shotgun away from him. He and his friends were then hustled
away so that the unpleasant business which brought us there could be
completed.

In due course I reported to the hospital to have the wound on my
head dressed but otherwise I tried to make light of the matter. The man
had obviously been under extreme pressure and clearly the tap on his
head had, in the circumstances, been inappropriate. I was, however, a
trifle surprised when a few days later the man appeared outside my

temporary office in the *boma* to await my command as though nothing untoward had happened. Unfortunately, a few days later word of the event reached my wife from someone in Lundazi who happened to ask if my head had healed and the story came out. She was horrified and marched in to see the District Commissioner, now returned to Fort Jimmy and in total ignorance of what had happened, to enquire what he proposed to do to protect me from what appeared to be a homicidal maniac. She and the District Commissioner were not reassured to discover that he was back on duty and sitting outside my office. There were more important things to deal with but I believe that he was transferred to duties which removed him from any temptation to hit me over the head again.

This, however, was only one example, admittedly of close personal interest, of a malaise that afflicted the whole area, namely the breakdown of law and order. I can confirm, from my own observation, that it is a thoroughly unnerving experience when all of the arrangements that society has put in place to prevent people from behaving like animals disintegrate and when the only thing that prevents a man being clubbed to death by his neighbour is the size of his own club and the speed and dexterity with which he uses it. The local population were nervy and went armed, and had every reason to do so. Perhaps my imagination was working overtime, but I felt there was an atmosphere of fear and menace in the air and, when we later ventured out of the *boma*, I felt sure I could smell the stench of death from the corpses of those who had been killed in revenge or to pay off old scores unconnected with the Lenshinas and which had been left out for the hyenas and other scavengers to dispose of.

The background to this was the fact that after the Chipoma operation everything ground to a halt, while those who had the unpleasant responsibility for the situation pondered what to do next. There were rumours that another band of Lenshinas were operating to the north of Lundazi, but those in authority seemed to hesitate to take steps to investigate those rumours. I cannot now remember whether the administration hesitated to allow the army to become involved again, with the possibility/probability of another bloodbath, or whether the army was reluctant to commit its soldiers to an advance some distance from the *boma* with insufficient force and intelligence. In any event there was a period when everything appeared to be in limbo and when I was reduced to undertaking such mundane tasks as rounding up the vehicles which the military had appropriated. Those who, like me, did not have the responsibility for the decision were, of course, full of complaints about the delay. Eventually the order was given for an advance in strength. I was included in the expedition, although on what conceivable basis I cannot now remember, bearing in mind that I did not know the area, did not speak the language and my Messengers (other than my driver Chicomeni) had wisely been returned to Fort Jimmy. In any event, when the army launched its advance in the early hours of the morning I went with them.

It was a long and extremely uncomfortable journey. It was very cold as, in the early hours of the morning, we started off in convoy over terrible roads. Very soon, however, the sun rose and it became unbearably hot and dusty. I was in a Land-Rover with one of the young European officers of the regiment. To avoid the possibility of ambush we were accompanied by a police spotter plane, which joined us soon after it became light. We advanced extremely slowly. I cannot remember that we passed any sign of life. Eventually in the early afternoon we received word from the spotter aircraft that there was something ahead that required investigation. He was correct. We came upon the village of Pishiku. It had clearly been a Lenshina village surrounded by a stockade. The stench was horrendous. The local villages had given up waiting for the government to act and had taken the law into their own hands and attacked the village and slaughtered and mutilated its inhabitants, men, women and children – around a hundred of them. Incredibly, although the attack had happened some days before, one woman, badly injured, survived. There was nothing useful that we could do except, with handkerchiefs over our faces to try to keep out the worst of the stench, to gather together the corpses and cremate them with petrol from our trucks. We crawled home sick at heart that our hesitation in advancing had allowed even more casualties and left antagonisms between the villages which it would take generations to mend.

The European population of Lundazi, I imagine, had never been very great and had clearly been run down in the expectation of Independence. Indeed, apart from the District Commissioner, who returned, fortunately unharmed, from his tour shortly after the operation in Chipoma, and his District Officer, I cannot remember any other Europeans in the town other than the couple in the 'Rumpelstiltskin' Castle Hotel. The hotel and particularly its bar naturally became the off-duty centre for those who had come in to deal with the Lenshina problem. Predominantly these were the army and police and in the evenings there would be an impressive array of Sten guns and sidearms stacked outside the bar. I think most of us, whether army, police or civilian, felt extremely unhappy with the situation and the part we were required to play in it. We were not at all reassured by the encouragement of the representatives of the African government in waiting to 'do our duty' in suppressing the Lenshina. In any event a considerable amount of beer was drunk of an evening. The bar was presided over by the female proprietor, assisted, unusually, by an African girl, whose behind was in more or less exact proportion to the front of her lady employer. The view down the bar from the side when the two ladies were on duty was one of the more remarkable sights of Central Africa.

One of the earliest arrivals was a charming elderly lady who, it subsequently emerged, was an exact contemporary of my mother-in-law at Oxford. She was in Lundazi as the representative of one of the relief agencies and her days, when she was not touring round the villages with a complete disregard for either her comfort or safety, were spent in the outbuilding that had been set aside for the purpose, sorting through the second-hand clothes that had been donated by a kindly British public for those requiring to be clothed. She was entirely at ease with the host of young army and police officers who frequented the bar, which she would patronise for a pre-prandial drink. The young men in turn were obviously fond of and comfortable with her. I came in one evening when the bar was packed and a sing-song was in full swing. As I came in, Miss Prenley and her modest glass of beer shandy were in imminent danger of being overwhelmed in the crush. A large young man, realising her difficulty, picked her up and placed her gently on the bar, from which point of vantage she led the hymn-singing, apparently oblivious to the fact that the words the young men were singing bore little resemblance to hers.

The male proprietor appeared to take little part in the running of the hotel. I felt sorry for the little man and got into conversation with him as a result of which I discovered that he had been a swimmer of some note in his young days in France. I asked him if he would like to give me some hints how to improve my swimming, a challenge which he seemed glad to accept. The result was that most of my spare time was spent in the excellent pool which the hotel boasted under his instruction (and no nonsense about it). Perhaps the only positive outcome of my time in Lundazi was my ability to perform a creditable imitation of a Pacific crawl.

Soon after the Pishiku operation the battalions of the Northern Rhodesia Regiment changed and, as it was thought the remnants of the Lenshina had crossed the Luangwa, presumably to link up with their coreligionists in the Northern Province, they moved down to the

*The police spotter plane in Lundazi.*

Luangwa. Again I went with them, though for what purpose or in what capacity I cannot now remember. Nor indeed do I remember that the Regiment did anything very exciting, although it did suffer its first, and as far as I am aware, only casualty when one of the young soldiers had to be evacuated as an emergency by air when he swallowed, while swimming, the metal lever off a ration tin of beer that was floating in the river.

I enjoyed being with the soldiers, who were jovial fellows, although there were rather a lot of them and they did shout a lot. It also allowed me to resume my acquaintance with the formidable figure of Regimental Sergeant Major Njobu whom I had met a month or so previously, when he was on leave back in his home village in the Kunda Valley, I believe in Chief Malama's area. I had been on tour and had found him taking his ease outside his hut. I think I had expressed some surprise that such an eminent gentleman should be one of my parishioners. Perhaps my expression revealed that I doubted his being what he said he was. In any event he had insisted on changing into his uniform and posing outside his hut between two elephant tusks, which was appropriate because his name *Njobu* meant 'Elephant' in Chinyanja. Whether this was his real name or whether it was out of deference to his bulk, which was considerable, or to his expertise in shooting them, I never found out. By what genetic kink the little Kunda had produced such a giant of a man I could not imagine. He seemed as pleased to see me as I was to see him and undoubtedly my acquaintance with him did wonders for my reputation amongst the soldiers.

I had by now been in Lundazi for some weeks and I had had very little contact with my wife in Fort Jimmy. I accordingly jumped at the chance to hitch a lift on a police spotter plane which was paying a visit to that town. There was no time or opportunity to send word to my wife. When we got to Fort Jimmy I asked the pilot to fly over my house in the hope that my wife would realise I was on board and come and collect me from the airfield which was some five miles out of town. There was no sign of life at the house and when I succeeded in getting a lift into town and up to the house, I discovered the reason for the lack of reaction was that my wife, aided and abetted by her mother, had decided that as a scion of an army family her place was in the front line. She had accordingly, and without any reference to me or indeed anyone else, commandeered a *boma* lorry, packed the whole of our goods and chattels on to it and had set out for Lundazi in our new Volkswagen Beetle. With her mother as passenger and with the lorry bringing up the rear, she was on her way to Lundazi at precisely the same time I was on my way to see them in Fort Jimmy. I returned in the spotter plane to Lundazi and we were soon installed in a spare Provincial Administration bungalow. For the remainder of my time in Lundazi I had all the comforts of home.

They had arrived just in time for my twenty-fifth birthday on the twenty-third of August. Shortly before this the new Provincial Commissioner had arrived without warning, so that there was no one to meet him off the aircraft, and it was entirely by chance that I happened to be passing the airfield on some errand and found him walking in the general direction of the town. I stopped and, when he told me who he was, I made haste to give him a lift to the *boma*. It emerged that he had been a Chindit during the war, and was therefore just the man to take charge of affairs and install into our operations a sense of direction, which recently, it had seemed to me, had been lacking. It was his insistence that the only way to defeat the Lenshinas was to get out into the bush on foot. By this time, and in the absence of anyone to shoot at, the army had withdrawn, leaving a platoon of the Police Mobile Unit to act under the direction of the Provincial Commissioner as a *masse de manoeuvre*, as I believe the French call it; in other words, an armed force to respond to any assault by the Lenshinas, which by now looked increasingly unlikely.

In the first instance the Provincial Commissioner directed that regular flights should be made by the police spotter plane over the Luangwa where the Lenshinas were thought to be lurking. A large, and no doubt competent, officer of the Mobile Unit had been recruited as the 'spotter' to sit in the back of the tiny aircraft, which was provided for the purpose, and look out for any Lenshinas skulking in the undergrowth of the river valley. Unfortunately the officer was so large as to make it virtually impossible for him to get into the aircraft, let alone move around sufficiently to keep a proper lookout. Even more seriously (from the pilot's point of view) he was not a good traveller and spent most of his time being sick. Authority accordingly cast about for a replacement and its eye fell upon me. Whereas the reasoning behind my appointment for my previous tasks in Lundazi had been shrouded in doubt, there was no doubt at all why I was chosen as a member of the police airborne reconnaissance team: I was very junior; I was not doing anything else (I had recently been reduced to carrying out an equipment check at the Castle Hotel); and, experience soon showed, I had a cast-iron stomach which was impervious to the movements of the little aircraft, which bounced around in the air pockets created by the hot air rising from the flat plain over which we flew.

Accordingly for the next few weeks I travelled in the back of the spotter plane as it flew, every dawn and sometimes last thing in the evening, from Lundazi airfield out over the escarpment and on over the wide valley through which the Luangwa meandered, in huge silver coils through wide sand banks. Part but by no means all of the valley was game reserve, and there were inhabited areas where there were villages, some of them quite large and all of them apparently deserted, presumably as a result of fear of an attack by the Lenshinas. We flew at either end of the day, in the hope that if the Lenshinas were hiding out in the valley, they might be tempted to light a fire or fires at night to cook their food, and to keep away the animals, which might be visible to us first thing in the morning or just before the sun set. We used, therefore, to bumble up and down the valley, bouncing around in every current of air trying to peer through the dawn mist or the evening heat haze looking, entirely unsuccessfully, for any sign of life. The pilots were both amateurs who had been recruited as police reservists for the duration of the troubles. The senior, called Mike, was the managing director of an earth moving company. The boredom was regularly relieved by our getting lost and then there were noisy exchanges as to where we were and whose fault it was that we did not know where we were. It was Mike who hit on the idea of using the Very pistol, which formed part of our safety equipment, to set fire to huts in the abandoned villages to try to flush out any Lenshinas who might be hiding in them. I had the starring role in this exercise.

When we found a village that we suspected might be hiding fugitive Lenshinas, I would get out of the seat at the rear, which faced forward in the same direction as the pilot and co-pilot seats. By turning round and crouching down behind the pilots' seats, I could see backwards through the little rear windows. We would climb to a thousand feet or so and then dive towards the suspect village. Towards the bottom of the dive, and in response to a call from the front, I would open one or other of the side doors and keep it open against the slipstream by stretching out a leg. I would then take up the Very pistol. Stretching out my arms and bracing myself backwards against the back of the pilot or co pilot's seat, I would try to hold the heavy weapon steady and pointing past my foot, the wing of the plane and the strut which, sprouting out from the body of the aircraft, supported the wing. As the aircraft levelled out at the bottom of the dive, I would wait until a hut or huts appeared briefly in the gap left by the open door and the underside of the wing, and then, attempting to lay off for the expected track of the projectile, I would pull the trigger and watch the thin trail of smoke as the round swooped towards the hut or huts below. The pilot would climb and turn so as to try to keep the target village in view and hoping to see either the hut catch fire and/or a startled Lenshina leaping for safety. No Lenshina ever appeared but we did succeed in setting huts alight sufficiently often to establish the negative, namely that the Lenshinas were not hiding in any of the abandoned villages. It also provided some welcome entertainment in what was becoming an increasingly monotonous exercise, although I do not imagine a modern Health and Safety Officer would approve. Only once did we see any sign of life and ironically it was on my last flight and on the one and only occasion that my wife flew with us.

Most mornings, after our flight, the two pilots would come along for breakfast at our bungalow and, in a gesture of thanks for my wife's hospitality, they pressed her to come with us on my last flight with them. She was naturally apprehensive that it might be necessary to indulge in the hair-raising operations that I had often, with some relish, described. The pilots promised, hands on heart, that they would fly straight and level so that she could, had she been minded to do so, hold a cup of tea unspilled on her lap. Authority had nothing to say about the invitation for the very good reason that Authority was not asked for its view on the appropriateness of allowing a civilian, and a female civilian to boot, to take a joy-ride in a police spotter aircraft over what was thought to be territory occupied by a vicious enemy. So it was that my wife was ensconced in the aircraft in the dark and as inconspicuously as possible and with strict orders to keep her head between her legs until we were airborne.

True to their word the pilot flew steady and straight out over the escarpment and over the valley which was just beginning to be lit by the rising sun. Just as my wife was starting to relax and enjoy the scene, one of the pilots pointed to what was, in effect, a copse of larger trees from which there appeared to be a thin pillar of smoke rising. Immediately he put the aircraft into a dive, to cover the ground towards the copse as quickly as possible. As we approached we all thought we could see some figures moving among the trees, but by the time we had flown past and turned for another pass over the copse, not only was there no sign of life but there was no longer any pillar of smoke, although we thought we could detect some wisps still lingering among the higher branches. As we prepared for another pass over the copse, it occurred to one of the pilots that although it was only a small aircraft, from the ground it would present a very large target if anyone down below possessed a rifle, as it was rumoured was the case. Just short of the little wood, the pilot accordingly threw the aircraft into a tight turn, and at the same time pulled its nose up, to gain a safe height. Having achieved this, we pondered what to do. Clearly it was our duty to investigate as much as we could, while at the same time exposing the aircraft, and for that matter ourselves, to as little danger as possible. The best way to do that was to dive out of the sun and then pull away as quickly as possible. With an apology to my wife for having to subject her to precisely the kind of manoeuvre she had feared, the pilot put the plane into a steep dive, pulling out and twisting away just above tree level. This was repeated over the next twenty minutes or so without producing any further sightings of anything suspicious and, as our fuel was getting low, we eventually took my relieved wife back to Lundazi. She escaped the indignity of being sick and even assisted in the preparation of our breakfast but it was noticeable that she seemed a trifle preoccupied and decided against eating anything herself.

That it was my last flight in the spotter plane was due to my being sent down to the Luangwa Valley, to join a platoon of the Police Mobile Unit that had been posted down there, presumably, to guard against the possibility of any further Lenshina incursion, either by the remnant of the Lenshinas who had fled from Lundazi or Pishiku and for whom we had been searching from the air, or from the Lenshina congregations in the Northern Province. It was part of the new Provincial Commissioner's philosophy that the only way to deal with the Lenshinas was to get in after them on the ground. Although he did not go so far as to send troops or police into the thick bush across the Luangwa to make contact with the Lenshinas, he did enthusiastically endorse a scheme for sending in two converted deacons of the Lenshina church, who had been found and bribed and browbeaten into 'volunteering' to slip across the Luangwa, to make contact with their co-religionists and then either persuade them to give themselves up, or failing that, return to report where the Lenshinas were hiding. It was felt, particularly by the officers of the Mobile Unit, for reasons that soon became very evident, that the interface with the deacons and any Lenshinas that the deacons might flush out, should be by someone not in uniform and preferably from the Provincial Administration. Although I did not speak the local language I, being young and with no other claims on my time, was the obvious choice for the role. And so immediately after my withdrawal from the spotter plane, I was dispatched in a Land-Rover, with the minimum of personal effects, to join the mobile unit in the Valley.

The spotter plane had not quite done with me, however. Soon after, we had descended from the escarpment and had started to bowl along the sandy tracks, across the Valley floor towards the Luangwa. We came around a corner and were confronted by the little aircraft landed, apparently unharmed, on the track, attended by my pilot friends, looking not a little shaken, and surrounded by a crowd of fascinated local villagers. Apparently some mechanical problem had overtaken them and it had needed a great deal of luck and some very clever flying to get them safely down on the track to the valley. Having checked that help was on the way, and with a warning against the dangers of flying without a member of the Provincial Administration on board, I proceeded on my way to join the Mobile Unit.

I found the platoon of the unit I was to be attached to camped in tents in the playground of a local school. The Police Mobile Unit, I should explain, were formed and used to control riots in the huge townships in the Copper Belt. There the explosive mixture of a largely male population, living in dormitories with their pockets full of money earned from the mines and with alcohol freely available in the township beer halls, was no doubt easily inflamed by the fiery oratory of the Nationalist parties into causing potentially serious trouble. To cope with this the Mobile Units (I forget how many platoons of them there were but I guess some four or five hundred men in all) were stationed in barracks amongst the mining towns. They were organised in platoons with European officers, many, I suspect, locally recruited, and African non-commissioned officers and constables. Although the men were nominally policemen with the same powers and in the same uniforms as ordinary policemen, their recruitment and training were very different. In the circumstances of their employment brawn was obviously more important than brains. They were very rigorously trained and disciplined and in the urban setting of the mine townships were obviously a formidable force. The constables were issued, in addition to the usual police handcuffs, staves and whistles, with steel helmets, riot shields and pickaxe helves. The officers and NCOs also carried a variety of firearms in case of emergency. They were not designed to be used in a normal police role or in open country and should never have been deployed in Lundazi where, in my humble opinion, a force of armed Messengers, who knew the local conditions and the local people, would have been more effective.

However, I found them to be charming people. Their senior officer called Brian, was, I think just for the purposes of their deployment in

Lundazi, an Assistant Superintendent but had been, until only a few years previously, a constable on the beat in Leeds. His enterprise in applying for an overseas contract had very properly been rewarded by promotion undreamed of in England. He was a most amusing companion and welcomed me into the tent, and the officer's mess and sleeping quarters that it housed. My role was soon explained to me. The two deacons had been delivered and they were only waiting for me to arrive to put the plan into effect. It was very simple. The platoon in full fighting gear would be taken in their lorries to an unloading point, half a mile from the river. They would then advance in open order, keeping a keen lookout for any possible ambush, to within two hundred yards of the river, where they would establish a defensive position. The deacons and I would then advance to the riverbank where I was to observe, preferably without being seen by any Lenshinas on the far bank, that the deacons did indeed cross the river and embark on what was clearly a pretty desperate mission. The process was to be repeated at every dusk and dawn for the next week, to receive the deacons if and when they returned. There were, I proposed, certain modifications to the scheme that occurred to me. Why should not at least a section of the platoon, all heavily armed, accompany me to the actual riverbank in case of the ambush which was so evidently feared.

'Oh no,' Brian assured me. 'A section would make far too much noise and anyway not even the Lenshinas would attack an officer of the Provincial Administration.'

'At least give me something to protect myself with, something light and inconspicuous like a Sten gun.'

He was adamant that I should go unarmed.

And so that evening we went in the lorries to a point, far enough away as we judged, for the noise of the engines not to be heard by any Lenshinas lurking across the river. The platoon then disembarked, in as much silence as could be achieved by some thirty large and heavily-armed Africans jumping off the backs of two lorries, and set off cautiously, with weapons at the ready (the platoon must I think have been issued with rifles for the purposes of the detachment). In the gathering darkness, and at a whispered word of command from Brian, the platoon lowered itself to the ground and formed a protective circle around the deacons and myself. The deacons were not a very prepossessing pair but I suppose in the circumstances they could hardly be expected to be at their best. They nodded in apparent understanding of Brian's final reminder that we would wait for them every dawn and dusk for a week. Brian patted me on the back reassuringly and then, more to the point, relented and gave me his service revolver, which he carried in addition to a Sten gun, but insisting that I should try not to show that I was armed. This seemed a fairly fatuous instruction bearing in mind the substantial size and weight of the weapon, but I did my best to tuck it into the waistband of my trousers. Placing my hand on it did give me some assurance as the deacons and I advanced gingerly to the riverbank. There was no sound other than the usual noises of the Bush. The exposed sandbars of the river showed no sign of life and the deacons slid without protest down the riverbank and disappeared into the gloom. I watched, until I could no longer see even the ripple of their crossing the river, and then retreated to rejoin the platoon where Brian was just beginning to be concerned that something had happened to me. I soon settled into the routine. Every morning and every evening we went to the riverbank and I made my lonely and happily uneventful walk. The remainder of the day we lounged around in the shade of our tent reading and gossiping and sleeping. We found a baby duiker or some similar kind of miniature buck and Brian derived enormous pleasure from playing with it and feeding it.

The deacons never did reappear. Whether they rejoined the Lenshinas or whether they were killed by them or whether they simply disappeared, we never discovered. The platoon was recalled, and I with it, to Lundazi and then moved without me back to the Copper Belt in preparation for the Independence celebrations at the end of October.

There was an amusing footnote to this episode. On my return to England I met up with my friend Brian, who had by then left the Police and returned to England where he had found a place at university to read Law with a view to becoming a barrister. He had not struck me as the academic type and I was surprised that he had found a university to take him on as a mature student. 'It was all due to you,' he volunteered. 'Because of my service background the university authorities decided to make an exception in my case to their usual entry requirements and, instead of sitting the entrance examinations, they simply required me to write an essay on any subject that took my fancy. I was at a complete loss to know what to write about and then I thought of your visits to the riverbank in Lundazi. I wrote a highly-coloured description of you creeping up to the riverbank with the rest of us hiding behind you. The examiners were bowled over by the drama of it and offered me a place.'

After this excursion and with the exception of a final farewell flight with my friends of the police reconnaissance flight, there was very little for me to do in Lundazi. My mother-in-law of whom, contrary to tradition, I was extremely fond, departed at the end of her holiday and I was as sorry as my wife to see her go.

Perhaps to keep me out of mischief for a few days or perhaps as some kind of reward for my endeavours, I was allowed to pay an official visit to the game camp on the Nyika Plateau, part of which, by some extraordinary quirk of administrative history, belonged to Northern Rhodesia, although the major part of the plateau was over the border in Nyasaland. It was, in fact, easier to get from Lundazi to the Northern Rhodesian part of the reserve by travelling through Nyasaland. Despite this absurdity the pleasant duty of supervising the camp fell to District Commissioner Lundazi. I imagine that in happier times the duty of making supervisory visits to the camp at weekends was one with which the District Commissioner would have felt it unfair to burden his juniors. In any event we jumped at the chance to visit the plateau of which we had heard so much. Our expectations were not disappointed. By some geographical aberration, the plateau (or at least the part we visited) was vast rolling moorland, complete with what appeared to be gorse and heather, and interspersed with little streams which tinkled over stones in the approved Scottish manner. It was also blissfully cool after the heat of the Luangwa Valley so that we needed to wear sweaters in the morning and evening. I cannot remember that my official duties in the reserve were very demanding. We were only there for a day or two but it made a wonderful break from the horrors of Lundazi.

My only remaining Fort Jimmy messenger was Chicomeni Banda, who acted as my driver. It was becoming obvious from his unhappy look that he was missing Fort Jameson. Matters came to a head a few days after our return from the Nyika plateau to which Chicomeni had come as our driver. Perhaps it was the contrast between the freedom of being a driver out on a 'jolly' and the dull routine of being back in the *boma* with the Lundazi Messengers, all of whom were strangers to him, that drove him uncharacteristically to drown his sorrows. The result, in any event, was that late one evening a Lundazi Land-Rover appeared outside our bungalow, with a seriously worried Lundazi Senior Messenger, who begged me to come and deal with Chicomeni. The Land-Rover had been converted to carry prisoners and the back was enclosed in heavy-duty wire mesh. Chicomeni was in the back with a prisoner who was cowering as close to the cab at the front as he could, to get away from Chicomeni, whose face was contorted in fury. Just what the prisoner had done to wind Chicomeni up to such an extent I never discovered. He had obviously been drinking and unless something was done very quickly something very nasty was going to happen to the prisoner. So far Chicomeni had apparently contented himself with uttering threats and giving the wretched man the occasional shove. Although there were several Lundazi Messengers, who got out of the cab at my approach, they were obviously very reluctant to volunteer to try to overpower him. Indeed, with Chicomeni in that mood, it would have taken half an army to do so. Thinking quickly, and relying on the fact that being under the influence of alcohol he would not be capable of much logical thought, I decided to pretend that nothing was the matter. I accordingly approached the rear of the vehicle and, as discreetly as possible, unlocked the door into the wire-enclosed rear, at the same time speaking in what I hoped were reassuring tones to Chicomeni, congratulating him on his arrest. With the door open I ordered him to get out and make his report. The other Messengers moved restlessly in the dark. 'At least in there he is out of trouble. If he kills the prisoner that is bad luck on the prisoner but at least he won't damage us,' I could imagine them thinking. Extraordinarily, however, and through the fog of his drink, the habit of discipline reasserted itself. Chicomeni tumbled out of the rear of the Land-Rover and, clapping his hat back on his head, he came to attention and made some kind of report. Again I congratulated him, this time saying that there was no need to keep on guard as the other Messengers could do that. Instead, I ordered that he should immediately go off duty and go straight to his hut to sleep. He saluted smartly and executed a more or less steady about-turn and marched off into the night. The next day I arranged for his immediate return to Fort Jameson without a stain on his record.

We followed him a few days later but only long enough for me to hand over to another young officer who was coming on transfer from Balovale in the South-Western Province. We also said our farewells. Neither Sampson nor Phiri had come with us to Lundazi. It would not have been fair on them to have taken them into another tribal area and particularly one that was in such uproar. To James I gave as a farewell present a handsome leather toilet set which I hoped would be appropriate to his dignity and make up for having failed to take him with me to Lundazi. Thereafter we travelled on to Ndola where I was to transfer from being a very new and insignificant member of the Provincial Administration to being a new and even more insignificant member of the Judiciary.

We spent some four weeks in Ndola (in another Government rest house) while I underwent some rudimentary training, sitting with an excellent African Resident Magistrate, prior to my formal appointment to sit on my own as a Resident Magistrate in my own right in Balovale and Kabompo Districts in the South-Western Province. It was while we were in Ndola that, on the 24 October 1964, Zambia became an Independent Republic within the Commonwealth and I put in my letter of resignation from the permanent and pensionable employment of the Colonial Service. It was already clear that there was to be no long-term future for expatriate officers in the Provincial Administration. Although the need for expatriate Resident Magistrates would last rather longer, I could foresee all kinds of situations in which a magistrate would be under pressure to produce the decision the executive wanted. Much better, I thought, to leave while the new administration and I were still on good terms and while I was still young enough to start a new career back in England.

CHAPTER 7

# Resident Magistrate

MY CAREER as a Resident Magistrate had begun just after the UNIP election success and as the end of my first three-year tour was at least in sight. Although I was reluctant to have to face up to it, I was going to have to decide whether to return for another tour under the new independent government or to make a fresh start. It was against that background that my father, who in Lusaka and from his lofty post in the interim government had his ear pretty close to the ground, telephoned to draw my attention to an item in the *Government Gazette*.

'I don't suppose you read the *Gazette*?'

'No!'

'You should. It sometimes has some most interesting items. I'll send you the *Gazette* for this month. Read the section advertising Government bursaries.'

I could extract nothing more from him but my father was not in the habit of making long-distance telephone calls unless it was important and so when, in due course, the *Gazette* arrived, I duly read as directed and found an advertisement offering a fully-funded three-year training course to read for the Bar in England, open to anyone with the most minimal qualifications who was willing to sign on after qualification for three years as a Resident Magistrate in the Republic of Zambia.

I telephoned my father.

'I've read the *Gazette* but couldn't find anything that would be relevant to me, except the bursaries for Resident Magistrates, which is obviously designed as part of the policy of recruiting local Africans.'

'Yes, but it doesn't say so and it can't say so, because the policy of the government is to be strictly non-racial. To disqualify you because you are European would be in breach of that policy. Apply for the bursary; even your degree will be miles ahead of what the local chaps have got.'

Accordingly, after minimal nagging from my father, I applied for a bursary and promptly forgot all about it under pressure of more urgent events. Out of the blue, however, I received a call to attend before the Chief Justice of Northern Rhodesia, a charming, well-meaning English lawyer, for interview at his chambers in the High Court building in

153

Lusaka. He sat at the head of the regulation interview table with two others.

'Why have you applied for this bursary, Goddard?'

'Because I want to be a barrister, Sir.'

'But you will have to sign on to come back for three years.'

'I know that, Sir.'

'You realise this bursary is not designed for people like you.'

'Why, Sir? Is there something wrong with my qualifications?'

'Don't be impertinent, Goddard.'

'I didn't intend to be, Sir.'

'It was not intended for European officers.'

'But it doesn't say so, Sir, and the government is meant to be multi-racial, Sir.'

The Chief Justice rose to his feet.

'The interview will stand adjourned for a few minutes. Goddard, come with me.'

The Chief Justice led me out to what was obviously his private office. He sat behind his desk and gestured me to sit opposite him. He picked up what I could see was a bible and held it, whether to summon up inspiration or a thunderbolt was not clear. I feared the worst. I recalled that he was reputed to be very devout. He explained most reasonably the difficulty I was putting him in by applying for a bursary which was intended for local Africans. I regretted causing him embarrassment but refused to withdraw my application and assured him that I would truly be happy to serve as a Resident Magistrate back in Zambia for a few years. There was a silence and then he asked if I would want to pursue my application if I were to be offered (no promises of course) the post of Resident Magistrate without a professional qualification.

I need to explain at this point that, although the District Commissioners and District Officers had acted as magistrates in their districts and, incidentally, as Courts of Appeal for the native Courts under the supervision of the professionally qualified judges of the High Court, it had been the practice for some years, as the cases became more complex and increasingly involved in politically-motivated crime, for there to be professionally-qualified Resident Magistrates appointed in the provincial headquarters and in the big Copper Belt towns. Typically they would be barristers with several years' call but by no means always with a Colonial Service background.

For the Chief Justice to suggest that a twenty-four-year-old with a rather shaky third-class law degree should be appointed a Resident

Magistrate with the criminal powers of Quarter Sessions and the civil powers of the County Court indicated the extent of his embarrassment. Bearing in mind the enormous promotion involved and the fact that my salary would nearly trebled, I replied to the effect that if anyone was crazy enough to offer me the post of Resident Magistrate, I would be crazy not to accept. So it was that a month or so later and immediately after Independence, I found myself propelled from the Eastern Province to the opposite side of the country to be a Resident Magistrate.

Balovale was a charming little outstation in the South-Western Province. It was a district headquarters, some three hundred miles, along an extremely badly corrugated earth road, from the provincial head-quarters at Solwezi. The pleasant bungalows of the civil servants were scattered, at a discreet distance from each other, under mature trees along a promontory formed by a bend in the river Zambezi. The more senior officers, amongst whom I was now numbered, partly as a result of my amazing escalation in station and partly as a result of the departure of many of the expatriate officers following Independence, were situated actually on the banks of the river. Kabompo, in contrast, was truly horrible, being no more than a substation to Balovale and an entirely unremarkable little township on the road between Solwezi and Balovale. It was just far enough away to prevent me travelling comfortably to and fro in one day, so that I always had to spend the night in its rest house each week or so when I sat in Kabompo.

Back in Balovale there was a pleasant *boma* a few hundred yards' walk under the trees from my bungalow. There I took over the old District Commissioner's Court at the rear of the *boma* complex. A little office was found for me, close enough to the court to enable me to withdraw with the minimum of delay to consider and write my decisions and the reasons for them. The supervision which the High Court exercised over the Resident Magistrates, and for that matter the supervision that I and others with a judicial function exercised over the native Courts, depended on the requirement to keep a written record of the court proceedings, including a summary of the reasons for all final and interlocutory decisions.

As far as I can remember there were no expatriate settlers other than missionaries, of whom I have no clear recollection, save that, most unusually, they were American. There had obviously at one time been a considerable expatriate population but as a result of Independence that had substantially reduced by the time I arrived there. There was a recently appointed young bachelor District Commissioner, a Cambridge man with a passion for football. He was a few years older than me and on his third tour and he took me under his wing, albeit sensitive to the fact that I was, in theory, though certainly not in practice, more or less his equal in rank. Without fail every week his 'poor old mum' would send him the local paper from his hometown so that he could follow the doings of the local football side. I had a picture of a dear little old lady hobbling on her stick to send him his newspaper each week until I saw a recent photo of her, which showed a vigorous dark-haired woman in her early fifties. David was the rock around which not just the little expatriate community of Balovale but also the recently promoted African civil servants revolved. David acted as steward, groundsman and barman to the Balovale Club, which was the social centre of the community.

In addition to David and my wife and me there was, as I recall, a European trader and his wife (an unusual presence this as most of the stores were run by Indians) and a limpid but charming man, rather older than David, whose department I cannot now remember. There were two doctors, one African and one Indian, and two enormous black South African nursing sisters from the hospital. There was also a very nice, but very wet, American student kind of person, who had something to do with the American mission, who kept telling us how homesick he was and how much he was missing his fiancée, whose photograph he showed us at regular intervals (a rather large lady, I recall, with a toothy grin and a lot of hair). Then there was Archie. Archie came from Leeds and was a mechanical engineer in the Public Works Department and could turn his hand to anything. Archie had been everywhere and had done everything. He was aged somewhere between fifty and seventy-five depending on the time of day and whether or not he had shaved.

Our lives revolved around our work, the club, which opened two or three times a week or when there were visitors, the tennis court and the weekly air flight in from the line of rail some five hundred miles away. The plane, a six-seater, if I recall correctly, came in once a week and the entire civil service population used to drift up, as if by chance, to the grass airstrip close to the *boma* at the appointed time each week to collect the post or the goods, if one was well enough off to afford to order them from the line of rail, or to see who had arrived. There was the memorable occasion when an attractive young lady arrived, for what reason we never discovered. David was all for putting her into the rest house until he was bullied by popular uproar into putting her up for a week himself. He wore a smile for a week thereafter but denied that his behaviour had been anything that would have brought a blush to his 'poor old mum's cheeks.'

My first case was in Kabompo. It involved the young District Officer Cadet who had been an assistant to the District Commissioner in Balovale and who had, coincidentally, been transferred to the Eastern Province to replace me when I transferred to the Judiciary. Unfortunately on his way by car to the Eastern Province he had run over and killed an African on the road near Kabompo. It was clearly an accident. The unfortunate pedestrian had been drinking and had wandered into the path of the District Officer's car. Unhappily the African District Commissioner who had been newly appointed to Kabompo had been an assistant to the previous European District Commissioner (as I subsequently heard) and there was said to have been bad blood between him and my successor. Being newly appointed in authority and with his enemy, as it were, delivered into his hand, he could not resist the temptation to prosecute my successor for causing death by dangerous driving. Who else could possibly conduct the preliminary hearing but the newly-appointed, (now) twenty-five-year-old Resident Magistrate of Balovale and Kabompo? No less a person than the Chief Superintendent of Police from Solwezi was appointed to prosecute, with the new and vengeful District Commissioner seated behind him to ensure he did his duty. My successor had taken the precaution of seeking legal advice from my colleague, the Resident Magistrate in Fort Jameson before whom, in my previous persona as District Officer Cadet, I had only recently appeared with a singular lack of distinction.

As the case was to be called at eight a.m. sharp we none of us had any alternative but to spend the night at the rest house in Kabompo, which consisted of some five or six double rooms with a kitchen and one largish sitting room-cum-dining room with one large dining room table. The system was that the government employed two or three servants to run the rest house which included a modest store of tins of meat and vegetables and tinned fruit and the like. The traveller could either bring his own stores or more usually buy what he fancied (if that is the right word) from the store and the servants would then for a modest fee cook them (again if that is the right word) and serve them. Usually one was delighted to have company in the rest house and the staff was used to travellers, usually civil servants, joining forces to share their food and the beer which they brought with them. They were not to know that the three European officers who shared the rest house that night were the prosecutor and the accused, and that the very young and very silent young man who perforce joined them for dinner at the same dining-room table was the Resident Magistrate who was to hear the case the next morning.

*New friends in Balovale.*

In the event I threw the case out, I think correctly, but not without a great deal of soul searching as to whether I was being over-influenced by loyalty to kith and kin. In fact I think the decision I made was the brave one. The easy decision would have been to refuse the various submissions my successor, with coaching from my colleague in Fort Jameson, made and send the case on for trial, leaving the High Court to make the decision. In any event the High Court saw no reason to overturn my decision when my case record went in for scrutiny.

All my cases after that seemed easy.

With all the confidence of a twenty-five-year-old, and with my very shaky knowledge of the law buttressed by a copy of Archbold's *Criminal Practice and Procedure* and a complete set of the *All-England Law Reports*, I soon settled into my judicial duties. I also had a copy of the Northern Rhodesia Criminal Code based on the Indian Code written, I believe, by Macaulay, (he of the *Lays of Ancient Rome* fame) Most of the law that I administered was criminal law and most of the cases I dealt with were pretty straightforward. With the notable exception I have just recounted, all of the criminal cases involved Africans. They had the option of speaking English but all elected to speak in the vernacular of which, coming from the other side of the country, I had no knowledge and so all of my cases were conducted through an interpreter, a clever little man with bad BO and a gammy leg. The prosecutor was the local African police inspector, a large and very nice man, who also spoke in English. The defendants were never legally represented, as they were beginning to be in the larger centres.

Although the vast majority of my cases were criminal I did have one civil case which starred Archie of the Public Works Department. Archie was supervising a building project for which, as usual, sun-dried mud bricks were used. These bricks were made by turning the bricks out of the moulds in which the mud had been packed on to a flat area to dry. For some time Archie had been driven to distraction by some goats, which regularly strayed onto the site and in the process trampled on and ruined his bricks, as they lay drying in the sun. Archie tried putting up fences but the goats got through everything he tried. He warned the owner of the goats to keep them under control, eventually threatening that if they trespassed on his site again he would shoot them. The owner of the goats, whether through idiocy or stubbornness or with an eye to the main chance, did nothing to restrain the goats and so on the next occasion Archie found the goats on the site, which coincided with his also having a rifle with him, he aimed in the general direction of the goats intending, I suspected, merely to frighten the owner and/or his goats; whatever his intentions, the fact is that one of the goats fell over, shot neatly through the head.

The first I knew of the matter was when the owner of the goats appeared at my office enquiring if he could take out a summons for damages against Archie for the death and injury caused to his goats. Two of them he alleged had been killed. The owner was a black version of Archie, with a speech defect which made him nearly as incomprehensible in the vernacular as Archie, with his strong Yorkshire accent, was in English. I tried to achieve a settlement, on the basis that if the owner could limit his claim to one goat, Archie might be persuaded to plead that he had shot the goat by accident, and would make a small ex gratia payment for the loss of the goat, which the owner had no doubt long since eaten. Neither would hear of such a pusillanimous solution. Archie was by now rather proud of his shot and had persuaded himself that he had indeed shot to kill.

The case duly came before me and was argued at great length. I particularly enjoyed Archie's cross-examination (or at least such parts of it as I could understand).

'Why did your goats come onto my site?'

'Why shouldn't they? My goats have always grazed there.'

'Because it is government property. Didn't you see the notice?'

'I can't read.'

'All right, but I came to warn you, didn't I?'

'I couldn't understand you.' (Which was probably true bearing in mind the obscurity of Archie's native woodnotes wild.)

'Anyway, how many goats do you say I damaged.'

'Two were killed.'

Archie's breast swelled with pride.

'Are you saying that my one shot went through one goat and killed another?'

'They were very thin goats, Sir!'

I found against Archie on the basis that we could not have him going around decimating the local goat population, but I limited the damages to the value of one goat. Archie was rather put out to begin with, but he obviously felt, correctly, that he had got the better of the exchanges in court and soon forgave me. This case was, however, very much the exception and the usual grist to my judicial mill was petty crime. As in most societies the world over, young males were the section of the population most likely to appear in the courts. There were no social enquiry reports or probation officers to tender advice but on the other hand the families, at least the mother, would invariably appear in court, moving forward, when her young sinner's case was called, to sit on the floor alongside the dock to share responsibility for his misdeeds and, no doubt, when a fine was the penalty, helping to find that as well. These parents were not inhibited in addressing the bench and would often volunteer helpful information impartially for and against their progeny. For more serious misdeeds when prison was not available, because of the age of the defendant, and in the absence of any other alternative, the only available penalty was six or eight strokes of the cane, administered by a very large prison officer on the bare back and buttocks of the offender, under the supervision of my friend, the Chief of Police.

The native population seemed to take to the English procedures with no trouble at all and were not at all reticent about having their say. Indeed, on occasions they obviously relished the opportunity to demonstrate their histrionic abilities before a captive audience. They also had a keen sense of justice and had the endearing habit of clapping if they agreed with the decision, sometimes surprisingly. I remember one case where an adult thief was accused of and admitted to a whole series of burglaries around his village. He could do no other as he was caught red-handed. To steal from his own village, and from people who had so little, was, I considered, a heinous crime. I said so and sentenced him to seven years in prison, an enormous penalty in relation to the usual tariff for theft and which required ratification from the High Court (which was in due course forthcoming). The accused was, on this occasion, accompanied not merely by his parents, but also by what appeared to be most of his clan. I was apprehensive as to what reaction I would get at this swingeing penalty. I need not have worried. Not only did the clan clap with considerable vigour, but their senior male member made me a vehement little speech, which my interpreter translated as being a thank you for imposing such a heavy penalty that the victims and their relatives would not find it necessary to impose their own penalty on the perpetrator and his family.

Every week or so I visited Kabompo, which I hated with a deep and bitter loathing. There was an awful atmosphere there. I felt lonely there as I had never felt, with much more reason, anywhere else in Africa. The crimes seemed to be so much more horrible there than in Balovale just up the road. I remember, for instance, an unlawful wounding that came before me. The evidence was that the accused and his 'brother' had been to a beer party. I put the word 'brother' in parenthesis because, with the African extended family, a brother was often not what we would regard as a brother with 'the same mother and the same father' as we used to ask to clarify the situation. On this occasion they truly were brothers, which made matters even worse. It was a commercial beer party, where the brewer of the beer was not extending hospitality to his friends and relations, but was charging so much per calabash for his beer. The two brothers drank heavily together until a quarrel arose as to whose turn it was to pay for the next calabash of beer. One brother pulled a knife on the other (a wicked home-made implement which I still use as a paper knife) and cut his brother's belly so that the intestines came out. My stomach turned. I tried to remain impassive as the gruesome facts were given to me in graphic detail, firstly by the police prosecutor and then by a mission doctor. After the stabbing a piece of sacking was found to hold the intestines together and then, when the victim appeared to be reluctant to die, those at the beer party decided they ought to try to get medical treatment for him. They accordingly concocted a home-made stretcher and set off across country, along the bush paths, several miles to the nearest road to find transport to take the man to hospital. In the event they were fortunate that the first vehicle that came along was a flatbed lorry from the local mission where there was a doctor. The patient was loaded on to the back of the lorry which had a considerable journey to get to the mission and the hospital there. That journey was over heavily corrugated roads in the heat of the day. The victim survived the journey and was patched up by the mission doctor, who came along with the man to appear before me only a matter of weeks after he was stabbed. The doctor made light of his part in the man's recovery, which he attributed to a divine providence and the man's incredible resilience.

Fortunately not all my crime was so 'heavy' and there were plenty of lighter moments, such as the embarrassing occasion when I came out of Court, having just imposed a heavy sentence on someone dealing in animal skins without a licence, which was a moderately serious offence, only to trip over my wife in the passage outside of the court concluding the purchase of a leopard skin from a shabby-looking individual, whose likelihood of holding a game dealer's licence was, I thought, pretty minimal. I cautioned my wife as to her conduct in similar terms to those I had used in court, but I had the distinct impression that it made considerably less impression of her than it had on the miscreant who had appeared rather more formally before me.

Then there was the occasion when I was hearing a case of goat rustling, which had to be adjourned in a hurry, because Dixon Oliver Goddard (definitely DOG on this occasion) was noisily harassing the goat which had been brought along as an exhibit and was tethered to a post outside the courthouse. Wisely, no one other than me was prepared to apprehend the dog. Dixon was what was called a standard dachshund but, like all dogs bred in the tropics, he had grown far larger and rangier than the European version. He was a splendid fellow, brave as a lion and with a sense of humour. Part of our large garden was a mango orchard and, during the mango season, was an irresistible attraction to the local small and not so small boys, who would choose the siesta period of the afternoon, when the government offices closed, to creep into our orchard to steal the fruit. On occasions, to deter this scrumping, Dixon and I would leave the house by the veranda door, the other side of the house to the orchard, and tiptoe round the side of the house to catch the boys up the trees. Dixon quickly learned the form and, instead of rushing on ahead, would patter alongside me and would peep around the corner of the house, as I did, to see if we were in luck. If there were boys up the trees he would wait until I gave the word and then streak forward, but delay barking, until he was virtually upon them. He obviously derived enormous satisfaction from seeing sometimes quite large boys leap for the safety of the branches. I often worried when the boys picked up a stone or a branch to threaten him, but to Dixon this was a bonus, and he would feint from side to side while advancing on his quarry, until the missile was thrown and then, dodging it, would dash in to snap at their ankles until they retreated to the trees. He was far too precious to leave behind and, when we left Balovale and returned to England, we flew him back with us.

I soon found that I had duties beyond sitting in court dealing with the criminal frailties of the local population. One of these was to adjudicate on those who were thought to be insane. This required an examination of the patient, over a period, by a properly-qualified medical practitioner, whose findings had to be confirmed by a second doctor. A joint application had then to be made to a duly appointed judicial officer, which meant, for the unfortunate insane of Balovale and Kabompo, me. For those who worked in the provinces, this procedure was thought an unnecessary waste of time as we could always tell who was insane, because they would allow their hair to grow in long Rastafarian style, which no self-respecting African would do, preferring to keep his hair cut short and clean and cool. Long Rastafarian hair indicated that there was no one who was willing, or able, to look after the poor unfortunate, because the family would usually look after anyone so afflicted, including making sure his hair was properly cut. However, the rules laid down a procedure and we had no alternative but to follow the procedure, irksome as we found it.

It was, of course, the doctors who complained most, as it was they who had to look after the poor wretch while they carried out their observations. They hit on a happy scheme, however, that on reflection I decided suited everyone very well and accorded with the best traditions of their profession. I took my motor car one day to the petrol pump at the hospital which, as usual for such pumps, required someone strong to manipulate a long lever to bring the petrol up from the tank. I was horrified to find that the pump operator, who was mopping and mowing through the window at me, had an enormous mat of hair and was shouting away to himself. He filled me up with petrol very competently, however, (someone else dealt with the paper work) but I still thought it appropriate to ask the African doctor about the man, and he confirmed at once that the fellow was indeed in hospital for observation. Was not the petrol pump in the hospital grounds and was he not competent at operating the pump and was he not serving a useful purpose, while he was being observed by the medical staff whenever they visited the pumps? In the fullness of time the poor fellow appeared before me in chambers with the doctors, bearing forms all testifying that he was undoubtedly insane. I duly committed him as requiring medical attention. I do not recall what happened to him. I suppose it depended on whether or not the doctors had a successor to operate the hospital petrol pump.

Another duty was to inspect the local prison. This duty, like so many others, had originally been undertaken by the officers of the Provincial Administration. David decided, however, that as most of the prisoners had very soon been sent there by me, there was a certain irony, which he very much enjoyed, in making me responsible for their welfare. Accordingly, on most Saturday mornings I would present myself, respectably clad, at the prison, which was not far from the *boma*. There the prisoners would be drawn up for my inspection, the number varying between half a dozen and a dozen depending, I suppose, on the success of the local constabulary in fighting crime. Everything, particularly the whitewash and including the prisoners, was always in immaculate order, but of course labour was never a problem. At the end of my visit I would ask if there were any complaints but there never were. In fact, a proper European prison officer found his way to Balovale while I was there. He had never been away from the line of rail before and to visit an outstation was a tremendous adventure. He had not realised, he confided in the club which had been opened in his honour, that there was a prison in Balovale nor indeed had he ever heard of Balovale at all until he came to look at the list of prisons for which he had now taken over responsibility from the Provincial Administration. Following Independence, the little out-station prisons that the District Commissioners had previously run had in the reorganisation that followed Independence been passed over to the prison service who had previously been responsible only for the big prisons in the provincial capitals and in the Copper Belt towns. I saw him the next day and he was terribly excited that he had found a pair of leg shackles in the prison store. He said he had never seen any before and he took some persuading that they were no longer used.

A potentially less welcome duty appeared early one morning, when I was enjoying the morning air and the view over the Zambezi, in the unlikely person of the wet American, holding the hand of one of the enormous black South African nursing sisters. She was a charming woman but was, at a conservative estimate, at least twice his weight and not far away from being twice his age. They had, I surmised, spent the night together and he was obviously bowled over by the experience. They were 'in lurv', he announced, and were determined to get married as soon as possible. They assumed I was the right person to do the necessary. It was a considerable relief to tell them that David and not I was authorised to conduct marriages. No one could persuade the young man to pause to think of the realities, of his fiancée in America or of the differences of age and culture. I attended the ceremony, which took place a week or so later in David's office. The bride and her friend appeared in pre-war frills and flounces, including, I distinctly remember, long white gloves, which for some reason they thought it appropriate to take on and off at various stages of the proceedings, thereby adding substantially to the time taken for what was otherwise a very brief ceremony. There was a gruesome reception in, I believe, a hall at the mission, which we all reluctantly attended, for as short a time as possible, to watch the two nurses, discarding finery and finesse with equal speed, make a determined attempt to get drunk as quickly and as completely as possible.

One of the other results of the transfer of duties from the Provincial Administration was that I took over as supervising officer for the native courts in the two districts. The local Chiefs sat with Assessors as judges in these courts, as they had always done, administering tribal custom. The Chiefs were paid an allowance by the government for this and their other traditional duties and the government also paid a salary to their Assessors. In exchange for this largesse the government insisted on the appointment of Court Clerks to keep a record of what went on and what decisions were taken and why. The District Officers were required to read these records to make sure that nothing too untoward was going on. I had in my time in the Kunda valley read hundreds of them. The vast majority of the cases were to do with family law, mainly divorce. Previously the wages and equipment of the Court Clerks were the responsibility of the native authorities but with reorganisation that duty now passed to the Ministry of Justice.

Although as a recently retired District Officer I knew all about Court Clerks, it very soon became clear that this knowledge was not shared by the Chief Justice and his staff in Lusaka in the Ministry of Justice. Just like the senior prison officer, who was surprised to find he had inherited a prison in Balovale, so the gentleman I eventually spoke to in the Ministry of Justice seemed equally bemused to find that he had native courts and native Court Clerks in Balovale and Kabompo for which his department were responsible. This discovery was immediately followed by a determination on his part to have as little to do with them as possible. As I was some hundreds of miles of very corrugated road away, it no doubt seemed to him very likely that that would be easy to achieve. Unfortunately for him, as soon as I discovered that I was to take over not just reading case records but also general responsibility for the Chiefs' courts in my area and their personnel, I called a meeting of all of the Court Clerks, some two dozen in all, with the intention of getting to know them and letting them know what I expected of them. That may have been my intention but the intention of the Clerks, as they vociferously explained, was to make clear what they expected of me. It was a very long list. It included the urgent need for replacement uniforms and stationery, particularly the special forms on which they were required to write the court reports. There were numerous other requests and complaints, all of which seemed eminently reasonable and none of which had received any action since the Chief Justice had taken over responsibility for the Chiefs' courts. I accordingly made a careful note of them and promised that I would bring them urgently to the attention of the appropriate people in Lusaka. It was clear from their looks that the Clerks had little hope of my being able to fulfil my promise, however well intentioned. Stung by this lack of confidence I determined to prove them wrong. I embarked on a campaign. Initially I wrote letters and, when that elicited either no response at all or else merely an acknowledgement, I resorted to telegrams and eventually the telephone. My telephone conversations with the courteous but evasive gentleman to whom I spoke became increasingly heated. Why, he enquired, was I the only Magistrate who was bothering him about these Clerks? I tried to explain that my more senior colleagues were probably as ignorant as he of the needs, indeed most likely the very existence, of native Court Clerks. I speculated that before long they would all be badgering him to satisfy the needs of their Clerks. That was a mistaken line to take, however. The thought that there were dozens, if not hundreds, more Clerks lurking out in the bushes just waiting to interrupt his peaceful existence obviously had a strong effect on him and he put the phone down with the briefest of apologies. I never succeeded in persuading him to speak to me again on the telephone.

The only thing left to be done was to go to Lusaka in person and try to get to see the Chief Justice who, I persuaded myself, would be horrified to hear how his department was ignoring the poor Court Clerks. I consulted David. He was not reassuring. He was not at all sure that the Chief Justice would place quite the same priority on looking after the native Court Clerks of Balovale and Kabompo as I did. He reminded me, although I needed no reminding, that leaving one's station without permission was an offence only slightly less heinous than rape and murder. There was, of course, no chance of my contact in the department voluntarily allowing me to come anywhere near him. I pondered the matter. I was determined not to be beat. Eventually I hit on the idea of sending a telegram on the instant that I started my journey, explaining that I had urgent and important matters to discuss with the Chief Justice and was on my way to see him. I would by that means claim correctly that I had missed the telegrams that my message would undoubtedly elicit. 'Do not. Repeat. Do not leave Balovale for whatever reason. Any disobedience of this order will result in immediate decapitation.'

I travelled hard and fast and arriving in Lusaka did not even pause to remove the dust of travel before presenting myself at the office of the Chief Justice. I was admitted to his presence after only a short wait. As at our previous meeting he was clasping a bible. Did he clasp a bible whenever he had a guest or only when I intruded into his life? Probably the latter, I thought, as I accepted his offer to sit down and tell him what it was that brought me so far to see him. I could detect no irony in his tone and I thought that perhaps the Ministry of Justice had different rules to the Provincial Administration about abandoning one's station. In any event I launched into my plea on behalf of my native courts in general and their Clerks in particular, to which he listened patiently, interrupting me after a minute or so to call in an elegant gentleman, from whose voice I recognised as being the reluctant recipient of my complaints on the telephone. He did not look best pleased to see me ensconced in the office of the Chief Justice and by all appearances to have his ear. I had thought it prudent, however, in my plea to refrain from any complaint about my treatment and I continued this policy. When I eventually ended, the Chief Justice volunteered that in truth his department was finding it difficult to absorb its new responsibilities and asked what I suggested. I diffidently (I hope) suggested the meetings and training courses I had started in Balovale and Kabompo and that there be a set allocation of equipment and uniforms for the court staff. These suggestions were so well received that I made bold to suggest that, if he would like to sign a requisition for the equipment I had asked for my Clerks, I would collect it from the central government stores and get on back with it to Balovale. I hinted, not wishing to test my luck too far, that some of the equipment on my list was negotiable. Requisition forms were obviously not commonly available in the offices of the Chief Justice and it was my friend of the telephone, who was by now looking positively urbane (no doubt at the possibility of getting rid of me) who suggested that the tedium of form finding and filling could easily be avoided by the Chief Justice signing a letter of authority to the Stores, which he quickly produced, authorising the bearer, Mr Goddard, to collect whatever he wanted for his Court Clerks. He even volunteered to telephone in advance to avoid any questioning of my blank cheque. I was profuse in my thanks. The Chief Justice waved them aside 'but don't leave your station again without my permission, will you?'

I assured him I would not.

I lost no time in taking my letter to the stores where the head storekeeper soon entered into the spirit of the thing and, as soon as he got the idea of the kind of equipment that I needed, started recommending items that had never occurred to me but which, on reflection, I was happy to agree were obviously essential to the well-being of a well-equipped Court Clerk. It was quite late in the day by the time that I had overloaded my Land-Rover and could decide what to do. It was too late to start out on the long journey back. Besides, a celebration of some kind was obviously in order. It was as I was considering this that I was hailed by none other than my friend Mike, of the police spotter plane in Lundazi, who was now safely back in Lusaka. We were delighted to meet each other in more pleasant circumstances. Mike was some years older than I and had a charming wife and a clutch of young teenage daughters. I told him about my venture and its successful outcome. He poured scorn on the idea of starting my journey back that day and on the alternative of staying at the government rest house, and instead insisted that I stay with him and that later that night I join him and his wife at a recently established nightclub. They even, for that purpose, arranged for a young nursing sister friend of theirs to come along to keep me company. I enjoyed the evening enormously. Exhilarated by the success of my mission, relieved that I had avoided any chastisement for abandoning my station and relaxed by the copious quantities of alcohol that Mike generously pumped into me, I set about enjoying the evening. My new friend the nursing sister and I danced every dance even though, having been out of civilisation of that kind of thing for the past several months, the music and the dance, the Twist, were new to me. I asked whose music the disco was playing. My partner looked surprised. 'I thought everyone had heard of the Beatles, even in Balovale!'

I set off back home the next morning. The journey seemed even longer than it had coming down. It was not helped by my headache from my unaccustomed partying. The Court Clerks were appropriately grateful, if surprised, by the equipment I heaped upon them.

I soon slipped back into the routine of Balovale and our modest entertainment at the club in company with David. Under his leadership the club was becoming an example of multi-racial harmony, being patronised not only by the European expatriate officers, both resident and visiting, as in the past, but now by the recently promoted Africans, both resident and visiting, with a leavening, if that is the right word, of the American missionaries. One of the features of the social life of the club was the Saturday night dances which I enjoyed very much, not just for the fun of dancing, but to watch the enthusiasm with which the African members took to the dance floor. The average European male, if he dances at all, does so preferably in the dark and certainly in the anonymity of a crowd. His African brother on the other hand seeks the limelight. His aim, when dancing, is to stand out from the crowd so that all can see and admire.

I had forgotten this difference in cultural mores when, shortly after my Lusaka escapade, David suggested that I might like to accompany him to the Grand Independence Ball which the African community were organising at the Welfare Hall, a large, whitewashed and tin-roofed building near the African township where our government clerks and drivers and the general population lived. We strolled down together and were warmly welcomed by various of our African friends and given a preferential position at the bar, where European beer was served. The hall was packed. It was very, very hot. Music, mainly European, was provided by some kind of quite sophisticated sound system. It was extremely loud. We settled down leaning against the bar, trying to communicate with each other, and with the friends who came up to greet us, by shouting in each other's ears.

The Master of Ceremonies then announced that those present could choose the music that was played if he or she would like to make a modest contribution per item to defray the cost of the evening. There did not seem to be any takers and so, to try to start them off, I proffered a small note which was received with some enthusiasm, as it was apparently sufficient to buy not merely one track but an entire record. What was my choice of record? the Master of Ceremonies boomed over the loud speakers. The hall fell silent to hear my choice. I was no expert on popular music. Inspiration came to me. It was noisy, it was fun, it was tuneful and it was new and showed that this scion of the establishment at least was 'with it'. 'Anything by the Beatles!' I shouted. There was a nervous pause while a search was made for a Beatles record. To my relief the record was found and the strains of 'A Hard Day's Night' rang out and I turned back to my drink, satisfied that my duty had been done. Alas no one was dancing. I looked around for the reason. The record stopped. In the silence it was loudly explained over the loudspeaker that as I had bought the record I, and only I, was allowed to dance and demonstrate my expertise. In vain did I waive my rights and encourage the expectant multitude to take to the floor. They would have none of it. Nothing would satisfy them but that the Resident Magistrate should put aside his false modesty and demonstrate his prowess on the dance floor. Even David, in between gales of laughter at my predicament, was remorseless. I protested that I had no partner. 'Take your pick!' the crowd roared, pushing forward a variety of giggling damsels who were trying to hide their faces in their hands. There was no escape. By now I had been eased on to the floor. The record was restarted. I advanced on the prettiest of the damsels. Her attempts to avoid me were thwarted by the crowd, who shut off her means of escape by closing behind her. I launched myself into the enthusiastic Twist, which I had so recently learned in Lusaka. It took no more than a few seconds for my little partner to pick up the rhythm and the rudiments of the dance and we were soon gyrating in what I considered to be a thoroughly professional fashion. Never have I had such an enthusiastic, not to say ecstatic, audience. They also soon picked up the rhythm and clapped us on. They then started to practise the movements themselves on the sidelines. At the end of the first track I made an attempt to leave the floor but the crowd formed an impenetrable wall and my partner and I had no alternative but to continue for another track and then another. I felt like the heroine in the ballet *The Red Shoes* who is forced to dance until she dies from exhaustion. It was horrendously hot. I was grateful for the slight breeze that blew around my nether regions whenever I gyrated towards the floor as the dance, or at least my version of it, required. The next time I lowered myself towards the floor I stole a glance between my legs, towards the rear and the source of the breeze was immediately and very obviously revealed as being a large rent in my trousers through which my white underpants protruded. This time at the end of the track I insisted that I be allowed to escape and, after thanking my partner, I rejoined David, who was enjoying my discomfort from the safety of the bar. He agreed that we had done our duty and that it was time to retire.

My court did not usually attract a large following; indeed, apart from those whose employment or arrest or family connection with the accused required them to be there, the court was usually empty. At the next sitting of my court, after my exhibition at the Grand Independence Ball, however, it was packed with an audience anxious to see of what other excesses I was capable. I was relieved that they were disappointed and the audience quickly disappeared.

Although the criminal law that I administered was English law, or at least the Northern Rhodesian/Zambian version of it, I had a choice so far as civil law was concerned as between English common law and local custom. As I had no knowledge of local custom, I would have to recruit a local expert to sit with me if I needed to administer local custom. This happened only once and coincidentally was my last case before leaving Balovale and the Colonial Service. It was a family case. The local tribe in Balovale were patrilineal, as opposed to the Kunda with whose strange customs I was more familiar, who operated a matrilineal system. In the patrilineal system, a woman belonged to her father until she was in effect purchased with what was euphemistically called a dowry by her husband and his family whereupon she and her progeny became the property of her intended and his family. Bearing in mind the obvious financial advantages to a father or uncle, as the case might be, of being involved in the woman's matrimonial arrangements, the men were less than enthusiastic about the women making their own arrangements, which tended to be more concerned with the personal attributes of their intended rather than his financial health and/or that of his family. However, girls will be girls and boys were very keen to be boys and there was a fairly steady stream of young men who appeared before the chiefs' courts summonsed by outraged fathers or uncles or indeed elderly husbands demanding compensation for the damage caused to their property.

Against this background I was initially intrigued, and then not a little anxious, when I was asked by one of the Chiefs to hear a claim for damages brought by an irate father against one of the recently promoted African civil servants. In fact I believe the request originated from the young man, who made no secret in the town that he had high hopes that the new young Resident Magistrate, familiar with English law, would be more sympathetic to his predicament than the Chief, in whose interest it was to protect the old system. I made quite sure that both parties were happy for me to deal with the case and that they understood that I was at liberty to administer either English Common Law or local custom. I recruited the Chief's Senior Assessor who sat with me on the Bench. The facts were very simple. Indeed, the condition of the young lady who attended court was evidence enough of the 'damage' and the young man was happy, and I suspect proud, to acknowledge his responsibility and was indeed very willing to marry the young lady and she him. The only issue was whether or not the young man had to pay her father for the privilege of doing so.

I reserved my judgement for a week, and in between packing up to go, I spent hours researching the English law on the subject in the *All-England Law Reports*. It was, I believe, the only occasion on which I ever referred to them. I found some splendid old cases about fathers being deprived of their daughters' services, but none of it I found entirely apposite and, in those circumstances (as I carefully noted in my case record for the benefit of the supervising Judge) I had no alternative but to turn to local custom as spelled out to me by the Assessor. I remember that the court was very crowded as I came in to deliver what was to be my last judgement. One half of the court was occupied by elderly gentlemen, obviously with daughters of their own, I guessed, by the rapt attention with which they listened to my lengthy written judgement. The other half of the court was occupied by well-dressed and obviously well-to-do young men of the same age and type and with the same inclinations as the young defendant. They listened with equal care as I explained that English law had no equivalent cause of action. This caused the young men to smirk. But, I went on, there was very clear local customary law, as expounded to me by the learned Assessor, on the subject which I was required to administer in the absence of any relevant English law. This customary law made clear that I must find that the father's property had indeed been damaged and he was entitled to be compensated for it. The going rate of compensation was, I knew, very affordable to the young defendant and his friends. I added that, as the case had been heard in the Resident Magistrate's Court which had far greater powers than the Chief's Court, it would be proper to order compensation at a much higher rate, appropriate to that senior court. I was sorry for the long faces of the young men but comforted myself with the reflection that it would not be long before they were fathers themselves, when they would come to see, if not the wisdom of my judgement, at least its advantages.

My final duty before leaving Balovale was to make a last visit to the prison. The prisoners were drawn up for inspection as usual. I explained that this was to be the last inspection that I would be making and I wished them well. When I had finished one of the prisoners took a step forward and, although a recent arrival, suggested that he might speak on behalf of all of them. I remembered the man well. He had appeared before me a few weeks previously charged with witchcraft. The Northern Rhodesian penal code, which the new government had accepted, was devastating in its logic. It said (in summary) that there is no such thing as witchcraft and therefore anyone who purports to practise witchcraft or claims to be a witch doctor was a fraud and was guilty of an offence. There were various classes of witch doctor including what were, in effect, herbalists, and very good some of them were reputed to be. The more usual operators were, however, witch finders and it was these that the law was designed to deter. The local villagers and their cattle were heir to an impressive panoply of ills, ranging from malaria, in all its manifestations, all kinds of bowel disorders brought on by bad food and dirty water, through to sleeping sickness in cattle. It was, however, far more satisfying to blame the sudden death of a child or of a cow on some enemy who had put a curse on them rather than on dirty water or bad veterinary practices. The remedy was also far more fun than having to dig a new well or take the advice of the veterinary assistant. The preferred remedy was to call in a witch doctor or finder, of which there were a considerable number, some with enormous reputations so that they were in demand for miles around. Their modus operandi varied in detail but in principle they all purported to be able to sniff out the witches who had been bringing death and destruction to the village or area. A great deal depended on the belief that could be inspired in the efficacy of the treatment and, no doubt working on the basis of the old adage if it tastes nasty it must do you good, considerable efforts were made by the witch finders to frighten the life out of the villagers at the witch finding meetings, which were attended by people from miles around, depending on the reputation of the witch doctor. I am not sure whether the witch doctor's fee was paid by the family or families who had suffered the disasters or by public subscription. Perhaps both.

These sessions were no doubt quite entertaining for the majority of the audience and for the afflicted family, who had the considerable satisfaction of having someone to blame for their misfortune. They were not, however, very jolly for the poor wretch who was identified as being the witch. The witch doctors were, however, very astute and/or very well informed and invariably identified the most unpopular or least influential inhabitant. Elderly single ladies, particularly those with a wicked tongue, were a favourite choice. On this occasion, however, the 'sniffer-out' of witches made the wrong choice and selected as his victim an old lady with connections who were either too fond or too frightened of her to allow her to be designated a witch, and despite the pressure of the rest of the village rallied to her defence and reported the matter to the police. Accordingly, in due course an impressive number of witnesses appeared before me to give a graphic account of the goings-on at the sniffing-out ceremony in which the accused played the leading role. It was by common consent a virtuoso performance.

Prior to this, however, the accused had been formally charged with professing to be a witch doctor or finder. He was in appearance rather non-descript, of medium height with an urbane manner, and it was difficult to imagine him cavorting around in animal skins, as the witnesses subsequently described. The charge put to him by the Police Inspector reading from the charge sheet and interpreted by the interpreter was that he had with intent to deceive represented himself as a witch finder contrary to clause XYZ of the criminal code. How did he plead – Guilty or Not Guilty? I was used to defendants being somewhat at a loss to understand what it was of which they were accused and I was quick to step in and try to explain the charge.

'The Policeman says you told people in the village that you were a witch doctor or witch finder who could sniff out witches.'

I heard the Interpreter use the word *nyanga* which, with variations, was the word for witch doctor all across Zambia.

The accused nodded as if pleased by a compliment.

'He says he is a witch doctor,' the Interpreter reported.

'Perhaps he thought you meant herbalist,' I said.

The Interpreter looked unconvinced.

'Anyway,' I announced, 'I will record a Not Guilty Plea' and noted my case record to this effect. Although the Police Inspector looked cynical, I had a suspicion he was not displeased to be able to call the numerous witnesses that he and his staff had obviously been at considerable pains to accumulate and whose evidence it took some two days to hear. At the conclusion of each witness's evidence, I asked the accused to stand up and I explained that he had the opportunity, if he wished, to ask the witness any questions about his or (mainly) her evidence. On each occasion he thanked me courteously for my kindness but declined the privilege, usually adding some graceful words of tribute to the witness for the way in which he or she had given her evidence. Eventually towards the end of the second day the prosecution evidence was completed and I addressed the accused in the dock.

'You now have the opportunity to tell me your side of the story. You can do this in two ways. You can either address me from the dock where you are standing now, in which case I will make a careful note of everything that you say but, because the Policeman cannot ask you any questions about your story, I may place less weight on what you say than if you go into the witness box and tell me your side of the story, in which case the Policeman will be able to ask you questions.'

The accused elected to address me from the witness box.

The Interpreter from long practice took over.

'What is your name?'

'Who is your chief?'

'What is your Village?'

'What is your occupation?'

I ignored the reply 'witch doctor' to the last of these standard questions and invited him to tell me his version of events, repeating that the essence of the offence was the holding out that he could sniff out witches. He thanked me for my assistance and confirmed that he did understand the charge. Even the likelihood of imprisonment would not deter him from telling the truth which was that he was indeed a witch doctor and adding words to the effect (no doubt with a view to the future) that he was rather proud of it. Even the Police Inspector decided without prompting that he did not need to cross-examine and even I decided that I need not reserve judgement in such an open and shut case. Alas for such presumption! I subsequently heard that the supervising judge had ordered a retrial – 'the learned magistrate having failed, in his case record, to warn himself about accepting, as corroboration of an admission, the evidence of witnesses, who despite their number were all accomplices.'

At the time that he stepped forward, as the natural leader of the Balovale criminal community, I had no idea that he was to be the only blot on my judicial escutcheon.

'On behalf of us all,' he said, 'we wish you a safe journey to England where we hope your studies will go well and that you will soon come back to be a judge amongst us again.'